ORCS WAR-FIGHTING MANUAL

Also by Den Patrick:

Elves War-Fighting Manual
Dwarves War-Fighting Manual

ORCS
WAR-FIGHTING MANUAL

Den Patrick

Illustrations by Andrew James

GOLLANCZ
LONDON

The right of Den Patrick to be identified
as the author of this work has been asserted by him in
accordance with the Copyright, Designs and Patents Act 1988.

First published in Great Britain in 2013 by Gollancz
An imprint of the Orion Publishing Group
Orion House, 5 Upper St Martin's Lane, London WC2H 9EA
An Hachette UK Company

A CIP catalogue record for this book is available
from the British Library

ISBN 978 0 575 13275 7

1 3 5 7 9 10 8 6 4 2

Typeset at The Spartan Press Ltd,
Lymington, Hants

Printed and bound in Great Britain by
Clays Ltd, St Ives plc

The Orion Publishing Group's policy is to use papers that
are natural, renewable and recyclable products and made
from wood grown in sustainable forests. The logging and
manufacturing processes are expected to conform to the
environmental regulations of the country of origin.

www.orionbooks.co.uk
www.gollancz.co.uk

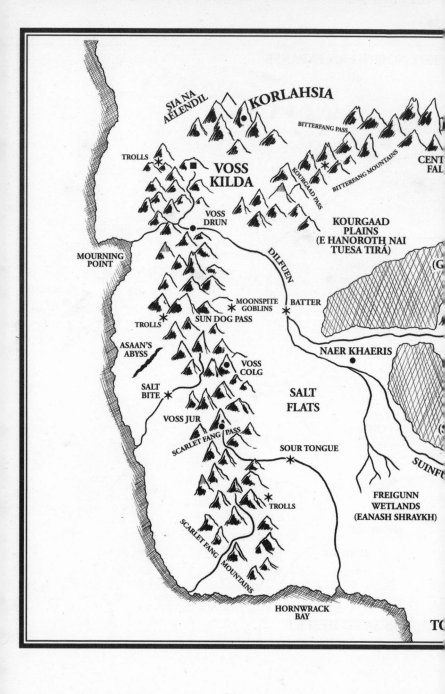

The Orc Harrowing

1

Beginnings

Back when the world was young there were no upright races; all were beasts. From the Bitterfang Mountains to the Diresand Desert not a single soul existed. Years passed and all was calm, from the jagged peaks of the Scarlet Fangs to the Silver Sea. Back at that time even the elements were at peace.

But that was to end.

The clever wind from the west grew restless. It whispered from the highest mountain top and breathed across the Salt Flats until it met the Great Forest. It swept the leaves from the trees and gathered the dust from the Kourgaad Plains. From this came the elves, and the wise west wind was the breath of life inside each of them. They sang and danced, learned to ride and harness the land to their wishes. They were swift, carefree and loved the open plains and deep forests, much as they do now.

Meanwhile, far to the south in the Diresand Desert, another force was at work. The long summers scorched the land and made all plants as kindling. Mirages and heat hazes shimmered above the dunes and made even the memory of water seem painfully distant. Great fires raged through the few woodlands of the south, sending up palls of smoke and burning ash. From these terrible and hungry flames came the orcs. They were restless and hot-blooded, consuming everything in their path, and were much as we are now.[1]

Later, the *daginn* would crudely fashion the dwarves from mindless clay, seeking to make an army of obedient servants for themselves.[2] But the *daginn* were careless and spilled the molten rock of the volcano into the clay. The dwarves became fiery and uncontrollable, liable to

1 Orc creation myths are perhaps the most numerous and most varied in all of Naer Evain. The elves have it that the orcs are corrupted men, wearing their lusts and mores on their faces for all to see. Humans, of course, widely believe that orcs are corrupted elves, twisted and ruined by their own self-pity. Dwarves tell of how the orcs are blights or cankers that swell in the mud and marshes of the world. They say Naer Evain herself spews them up like a sickness. The orc creation myth seems to change from culture to culture, and even appears to alter every decade or so. Most orcs don't really care about their creation myths. 'We're here, aren't we?' is the common response to any questions regarding their origins. Only orc shamans seem much concerned with the origins of their kin.

2 *Daginn* are found in orc myths or folk tales. Apparently they are giant winged wyrms that live near volcanoes, desolating the countryside nearby and sleeping on huge beds of golden coins. These myths are consistent in many ways with the *aelfir* belief in such creatures. The *daginn* are also referenced by the dwarves, who call them the great drakes. The huge piles of treasure are especially prevalent in dwarf folk lore.

terrible tempers once wronged. Proud and stubborn, the dwarves rebelled against their draconic masters, soon leaving the volcanoes where the *daginn* make their stony dens. The dwarves built mighty halls and impregnable fortresses to shelter from the rain. They hoarded their bright gold and shining gems like the *daginn* who made them, and continue to do so all these years later.

Wind, fire and earth. Three elements indifferent to each other. Wind can extinguish fire, but it can also fan small flames into ferocious infernos. Fire may scorch and blacken fertile ground, but sand and stone can stop the flames from taking hold. Earth seems impervious to gales and tornadoes, yet dust can be swept many miles. Wind, fire and earth, three elements bound to compete against each other for all of time, just as the orcs, dwarves and elves will fight a never-ending war, spilling blood across Naer Evain for ever.

ThE MiDDLE TiMES AND LESSER RACES

Goblins too came, after a time. Some crawled from dark places, others trekked up from the south, and still more emerged from the forests where they had remained hidden from the sun. They were small and insubstantial but shared many traits with the orcs.[3] Neither as impressive nor as all-consuming as their larger kin, they

3 'Goblin' in the orc tongue is closely related to the word for ember, or cinder. This is another reminder that the orcs identify closely with the element of fire and also consider goblins an offshoot of their own race. Elves on the other hand are called 'Onse' after the name of the west wind. This is usually prefixed by the letter 'p' when orcs pronounce it. I never learned why.

made their homes in the mountains. Here they sought to unseat the dwarves from their fortresses, as foolish an aim as arguing with an incoming tide. In time the goblins became allies of the orcs. And occasionally dinner.

And finally there were humans, who ventured down from the Northern Expanse. A rare few emerged from the Diresand Desert, but for the most part they arrived from the north, clad in furs and sporting small beards. Humans are not wind or fire or earth. Nor are they mixtures of these elements. Humans simply exist to annoy, providing food for any orc who can spare the time to hack them out of their armour. Weaker than an orc, less useful than a dwarf, less wise than an elf, more untrustworthy than a goblin. Humans really are the most pitiful race in all of Naer Evain. They shame themselves by selling their swords and reveal a lack of honour no orc could live with.[4]

OUR pLACE

We orcs have always been shunned by the other races. We are not diplomats, nor are we great craftsmen. We are not concerned with beauty like the elf, nor consumed by avarice like the dwarf. We are not afeared like the goblins, nor do we plot like the humans. Our purpose is simply to survive. We live to make war and expand the territory we control. We live to make names for ourselves

4 This is a reference to the human bandit companies who do indeed seek employment by orc tribes. While the orcs will happily use human mercenaries they generally distrust and despise them. This made my job practically untenable until I wangled myself the title of '*Khagan*'s Scribe'.

and to be remembered at the fireside during Great Feast and Midwinter.[5] We do not expect a peaceful existence with the other races because we have only ever known them as enemies.

At first we were frightened of the elves, thinking them strange forest spirits or phantoms in the night. Surely no living creature could move so quickly and with such grace, we thought. We hunted them down as best we could and they in turn left many of our kin face down in the mud with arrows through their hearts. But the elves are not spirits, they are made of flesh and blood just as we are. They are capable of fear and they can bleed. They can be caught and they can be killed. The proud elves think themselves above the concerns of the mortal races, but their endless longevity gives no meaning to their lives. By contrast, every orc knows his time is measured, and seeks to accomplish something with the few years he has.[6]

The dwarves are naturally given to suspicion and loathing. They have always turned us away from the shelter of the mountains. They seek to keep the mysteries of stone and metal to themselves. Only the ferocious

5 Great Feast is roughly equivalent to a harvest festival for the orcs, although it can occur at any time of year, usually after the sacking of a large town. Midwinter, by contrast, is always observed on the shortest day of the year.

6 This passage makes orcs sound short-lived, which is not true. None of the orcs I spoke to could recall any of their kin dying from old age. Cause of death was always war, or a brawl that went too far. Some suggest this longevity (such as it is) may be due to their horrific diet. However, I believe orcs fail to die of old age simply because it does not occur to them to do so.

akuun and the *daginn* refuse to give ground to the implacable dwarf.[7] Even now, our goblin kin find themselves in conflict with the greedy dwarves in the mines and tunnels. Testament to dwarven greed is the road they have laid across the great plains, a vein to feed their need for trade and gold. Happily, we orcs can plunder and lay waste the slow moving caravans, full of good food and bright, sharp steel.

The humans, most weak and mean of all the races, lie and twist words to their own satisfaction. They lack even the honesty to make alliances hold fast. We orcs are renowned for making war on each other, but it is always under the spirit of Harrowing.[8] Humans care less for fame than they do for power, wanting only to subjugate their fellow man. They are not as nimble as the elf, not as tenacious as the dwarf and lack the orc appetite for violence. If they serve any use at all, it is one that does not register in the orc mind. They are at best cattle and are not to be trusted when employed as mercenaries. Be sure to assign a fearsome orc to watch over any humans in your company; gold alone does not ensure loyalty.

---

7 *Akuun* is the orc word for mountain troll. More information on these frightful creatures can be found in Chapter 8.

8 Harrowing is a term used by orcs to describe any period of warfare or bloodshed. These conflicts are specifically to gain territory or raid resources and include a code of conduct. Orcs find the idea of assassinating each other for political gain completely alien and unthinkable. The literal translation of the word assassination in the orc tongue is a contraction of the words 'dagger human not friend'.

the great mother

We are quite separate from every living thing in the world. The *akuun* can match the call to violence we feel, but they are feeble-minded and slow. They are no better than beasts and have no interests beyond their own hunger.

The goblins have always been weaker than we orcs. They are cunning and cruel but only keen to attack when their numbers are vast and uncountable. Their ambitions are limited to stealing from the dwarves and little else. Wiser than the *akuun*, more fierce than the goblins, we orcs are quite alone in the world. And yet it need not have always been this way.

When the night sky gave up its most precious jewel we were compelled to seek her. In her own way Khaeris, Star of the West, is much like us, the fire of all fires. For many years she had looked down on us from the darkness, bathing us with her magnificent silver fire. Then, for reasons not clear to us, she collided with the earth, almost tearing the continent in two. An intense curiosity fired the hearts of orcs; a nameless desire to meet and hail the fire of all fires. Many tribes sent ambassadors and speakers to the forest, seeking an audience with the Great Mother. Shamans and the wisest orcs were sent with gifts of spices and prized wolves. Our women took the young and the sick, seeking the healing touch of the mysterious Goddess from the night sky. But all were slain. All were found run through with elven arrows, or else cut down after trekking no more than a handful of miles into the Great Forest. We were turned away, denied our chance to

meet with the most sacred of beings.[9] A thousand years we sought her, and for a thousand years we were turned back.

This is why we hunt the elves so implacably. What right have they to guard the secrets of the Goddess from the night sky? What right have they to declare themselves the only heirs to her teachings? What right do they have to deny us even the glimpse of the Great Mother? This is the grievance that drives the orc to war. It is all we have ever known; some say it is all we are good at. Where the dwarf jealously guards the mountains, we siege and sack. Where the elf protects his beloved woodland, we burn and defile. Where the human settles, we destroy.

Asaan Firebringer knew the place of the orc in the world. We should rule mountain and forest and plains and river. Let no corner of the world not know our presence, let no valley or hill go undiscovered.

We are the orcs and this world will belong to us.

* * *

Translated from the speech of Midwinter by Kani Break-speare, Ur-Khagan *of the Scarsfaalen tribes.*

– V.

9 If my translations match up it would seem the orcs were never granted access to the divine being called Khaeris. The elves' own historical record on this matter is vague at best.

2

THE HARROWING

It was only after several months that I felt able to ask Kani Breakspeare to explain the Harrowing to me. The Harrowing is the loose code the orcs follow, enshrining the values they adhere to. By that point I had been the Ur-Khagan's scribe for a good while, and, while not accepted, I was at least largely ignored by most of the orcs in the tribe. This was certainly preferable to orcs paying attention to me, which I was very grateful for. As Kani spoke that day he gathered quite a crowd, who were fascinated by his explanation.

– V.

WANDERING FLAMES

Light one small flame at the edge of a dry forest and watch it wander. It multiplies and moves, consuming the wood in its path. In time it creeps onto the plains and heath, burning the shrubs and grasses. All that is left behind is ash and blackened earth. And so it is to be an orc. If we stay still we dwindle and die, but with the wind at our back and fuel before us we can burn for eternity.

We orcs don't settle down. Not like other races. Sure, there are those orcs what live at the Great Meets, blacksmithing, tanning leather for armour or trading food. But they ain't real orcs. To be an orc is to be master of the world. We don't have borders or Kingdoms because all the world belongs to us, not just the *Khagan* either.[1] All the world belongs to all the orcs, from the most snot-nosed young 'un to the mightiest *Ur-Khagan*. The mountains are ours, the plains are ours, the rivers are ours, even the forests are ours, although we haven't quite persuaded the elves of that *yet*.

CONDUCT BETWEEN TRIBES

A proper orc likes a scrap. It's nothing personal, but if you've got something we need, then we're going to take it from you. There's nothing dishonest about this. You have the right to defend yourself and your things. Food, weapons, armour, wood – it's all the same. The stronger

---

1 Orcs don't have borders because they don't have maps, they don't have maps because they can't read. Kani did attempt to learn to read while I lived with the tribe, but he did it in secret. When I asked why, he replied, 'If the tribe see me doing something the elves do, they'll think I've lost me edge and kick me out.'

will ultimately own what is being fought over and the weaker will die. That's just life.[2]

This is all well and good to a point, especially if you can kill some elves while you're about it, but orcs need to be mindful of each other. Orcs killing orcs when we could be killing elves or dwarves is arseheaded.[3] For this reason we tend to avoid fighting and stealing between our tribes when we can. Not saying it doesn't happen. Some tribes are notorious for it. The best way for an orc to stay dangerous is to keep fighting. You ain't going to be much of a fighter if you're not constantly testing yourself. In the past this meant tribe on tribe warfare, but these days we try to reserve the kicking for other races.[4] Only at the Great Meets is fighting banned outright. I mean we have brawls, but they're only with fists and knives. Proper weapons get put in a wagon and tied up with rope.

It's bad form to attack a tribe leaving or journeying to a Greet Meet. If you can see the Meet on the horizon you should hold off on the kicking, is what I always say. A Meet is the one place a *Khagan* can relax a bit and focus his mind

2 The survival of the strongest is a common theme of orc life. Crippled orcs live out their days at the Great Meets, while orcs born with deficiencies are simply left in the wilds to perish. The small number of orc philosophers (mainly shamans) call this thinking Der Win Izm.

3 This is the literal translation of the orc word and as such requires little explanation. It is possibly one of the finest insults I have come across, in any language, in all of Naer Evain.

4 'Kicking' or 'the kicking' is roughly the same as scrapping or fighting: armed combat in order to steal supplies. Only 'brawling' is different, which is a regular occurrence among orcs, even those who might be considered friends or relatives. Note: 'kicking' is not the same as 'arse-kicking' which I describe later.

on trading and food. He doesn't want to be concerned with defending his gear from other tribes. That's why we don't fight within sight of a Great Meet. And you never, never attack young 'uns.[5] They're crap in a fight anyway, so it's no fun. Orcs killing young 'uns is an affront to the world, and damages the chances of us overrunning the other races. Once an orc kills a young 'un he's no better than a *Khast*, and should be dealt with in the same way.[6]

Female orcs are a different matter. Most of them are more dangerous that some of my own retinue, and crazier than some berserkers I've met. Others can give you the eye, which is bad news and to be avoided.[7]

5 The term 'young 'un' refers to any orc that appears to be under ten years old, according to Kani Breakspeare. Many orcs disagree and claim young 'uns are orcs under twelve. When asked how they'd verify an infant's age no one had much of an answer. This is another example of how orcs are much more invested in the argument than the solution. And a good argument will lead to someone getting a beating if it goes far enough. In this case it was very nearly me.

6 Orcs are obsessed with the idea of night spirits who prey on sleeping orcs. The orc wakes, changed irrevocably. He hungers after flesh, living and dead. Only shamans seem to be able to protect the orcs from these night spirits, which adds to their influence. It is my thinking that the Umber Wraiths have a part to play in this. The orcs consider *Khasts* to be the ultimate blasphemy, and go to great lengths to kill the corrupted creatures. More detail on *Khasts* is provided in Chapter 6.

7 Orcs are painfully superstitious. Salt plays a big part in their lives and it is believed to ward off fell spirits. Female orcs are regarded with grudging respect that often gives way to a deep wariness. It is said they can curse an orc with the evil eye, which dooms an orc with bad luck. I, of course, never had this problem. Anyway, I couldn't tell one gender from the other the whole time I lived among them.

Becoming Khagan

Any orc, male or female, can become the *Khagan* of a tribe. It's dead simple. An orc belonging to the tribe can challenge the existing *Khagan* at any time. Any time except in the middle of a raid or battle. That would just get confusing. Challenging a wounded *Khagan* is the mark of a coward, and those orcs who come to power like this rarely last long. Most tribes have a week of preparation for the challenge. Orcs don't like change, so it's good to give a few days' notice to everyone. That and the chance for everyone to lay bets – some orcs do well out of a challenge without ever drawing steel.

Leadership challenges are fought in a circle determined by the tribe shaman, usually about fifty feet wide. A proper challenge circle is laid on packed earth. Grass is for elves and rock is for goblins. Good dusty earth is best for this sort of fighting. The edge of the circle is ringed with salt to keep out any sorcery or fell influences. All boons and fetishes from shamans are banned: the challenge is strictly a feat of arms.[8] The tribe crowd around for a good look, because the next best thing to being in a scrap is watching one. The existing *Khagan* and the challenger face off against each other and fight with weapons chosen at random. Except for a longbow or crossbow, of course. No one is going to respect a *Khagan* who won a challenge with one of those. Besides, you might end up shooting an orc in the crowd, and then it

8 I lost track of the number of 'lucky fangs' the orcs wore, or raven feathers that supposedly imbued the orc with greater speed. The shamans do a brisk trade in inventing mystical trinkets that appeal to the orc sense of wonder.

will really kick off. The fight is to first blood, most of the time. Fighting to second blood is being thorough, to my mind, but fighting to third blood is just showing that you've gone a bit berserker. Sometimes a challenge goes to fourth blood, and a few times there is a burial the same week.[9] A wise *Khagan* won't kill without good reason. Killing challengers sends out the message that brutality is not just reserved for other races, but for anyone who ain't you. Quickest way to lose respect. Tribes led by this sort of *Khagan* drift apart quick. Pretty soon it's just a retinue with a lunatic leading it.

By fighting to first blood you retain the skills of the challenger. Your opponent gets a bit of prestige because there ain't no shame in losing to the *Khagan*. This new-found status comes in handy when you promote him to *Khagi* a few months later. Better to have an ambitious orc taking orders from you, rather than beating him in front of the tribe and leaving him kicking his arse.[10] However, a disrespectful challenger is asking for it. I like to decapitate them and use their head for a tent decoration. A disrespectful challenger is going to try to kill you to make his point. Everyone in the tribe knows this, so there's no loss of face if you finish him off. I like to

9 This idea of attaining leadership through challenge, while horrific to me at first, does ensure a certain amount of ambition and hope from orcs starting out on a lifetime of warfare. There are no lines of succession, no petty politicking, no alliances or betrayals.

10 I asked Kani if he meant 'kicking his heels', an idiom well known in Hoim to describe impatience or boredom. He looked at me and muttered, 'You think I don't know my foot from my arse?' I decided that although anatomically different, the expressions mean much the same thing.

make them suffer a bit too, but don't drag it out too long. Most times these challengers are put up by a shaman who's attempting to have one of their followers made *Khagan*. This does the tribe no good at all. Shaman business and *Khagan* business, while having common goals, usually follow different paths. One thing ain't like the other. A respectful challenger shows he's at one with the customs of the orcs. It's this attitude that makes him a good prospect for leadership. You want to keep orcs like this alive.

The *Khagan* also has the option of retiring with no loss of face. Sometimes you have to accept you're beaten. You might be too old, too wounded, or simply have had enough. Sometimes the best *Khagan* ain't the best fighter, so you need to be on your guard when a good fighter gets ambitious. Being *Khagan* is hard work and you get few if any thanks for it. It's worth remembering that you can retire and name a successor. You are *Khagan* after all. This successor will need to be on his guard – he'll be challenged within the first three months of his rule. I don't know why this is, but I think the idea of getting a new *Khagan* without a bloody great fight offends most orcs.

pRisoNeRs

Every *Khagan* has slightly different ideas about what to do with prisoners. Mine are probably a bit complicated, but I've heard they're becoming quite popular with the other tribes. Here's what I like to do.

Elves are bastards. It's a salt wind that blows at your back if you let elf prisoners walk free. They're tricksy and dangerous and you'll likely find yourself facing them again in a few years. Difficult to tell, of course, because they all look the same to me. It's important that elves know we'll kill them – keeps them in their forests and makes sure they don't get ideas about spreading out. It's also important to kill elves on account of all the females and young 'uns they killed when the Great Mother fell from the sky. It's not the orc way to hold on to grudges – they're the domain of dwarves – but some things can't go unanswered. I like to tie an elf to a tree and set fire to the whole thing. Some orcs will eat elf, but I'd rather go hungry than admit to eating the arrogant bastards.[11] They've got a sour aftertaste and repeat on me for days.

I've got into the habit of ransoming dwarves back to their citadels. Orcs used to tell me this was against the spirit of the Harrowing, but there's a reason for the ransom. Obviously you don't ask for money; that's nonsense. Instead ask for good dwarf steel. Naturally you get your retinue to piss all over the dwarf before you send him back. If he's a bit mouthy, you can cut his beard off too. Of course, capturing a dwarf is another matter entirely, and you might lose a few goblin messengers during the negotiations; but that's a small price to pay for some steel. If the ransom goes unpaid then you've always got a bit more meat for the pot. The other reason I like to ransom them is because dwarves are the best fighters in all of Naer Evain, except orcs, of course. If we

11 This caused quite a lot of friction in the tribes under Kani Breakspeare's command. Many were severely unhappy about not eating elves. Kani, however, was resolute and focused his raids on human farmsteads in the Arendsonn Kingdom instead.

let all the dwarves die we'd go soft, so they're good for us in a way. They make sure we don't lose our edge.

Humans are sod all use for anything.[12] Annoyingly they're the one race you're most likely to end up capturing. There's something pathetic about humans that means they give up when they're outnumbered. Dwarves will fight to the last man, smashing up all the kneecaps he can reach. Even the pansy elves stick it out, although they like to weep as they fight and sing those horrible high-pitched songs. Humans, though – no resolve. They'll drop their weapons, shit their pants, and expect to be let off with a light kicking. Not a chance.

Orcs like meat. Cows, chickens, pigs and boars. All very good. It's the meat that helps build muscle, and it's the muscle that helps us beat the piss out of the other races. Humans have quite a sweet flavour, not unlike good pig, and that's why we like raiding their farms so much. Some old-fashioned orcs say they'd rather not eat anything they didn't respect. That's all well and good when you're a single tribe, but when you're commanding three or four tribes and invading a town, there ain't going to be enough pigs and cows in all of Naer Evain. You've got to fill up on meat wherever you find it.[13]

12 Kani would often say this as if unaware that I was human myself. In time, I barely noticed when Kani would slander humans, instead nodding sagely and agreeing with him. Note: living among orcs does strange things to a man's mind.

13 Some orcs would eat the fallen human mercenaries they had employed to fight alongside them. This provided a huge incentive to me to stay alive, especially as I'd rather like to be interred in the family vault if Father ever forgives me.

BLOODY GOBLINS

Sneaking about at night time, sabotaging siege engines, and ambushing messengers are the hallmarks of a creature with no respect.[14] No respect for himself and no respect for his enemy. It's no way to do war.

When the enemy leader sends small groups of soldiers to hunt the *Khagan* he is, in fact, telling you something. He's declaring his soldiers are too cowardly for a proper, large-scale battle. Just like the elves to try to avoid a real fight with witchery and sneaking. Watch the humans try to copy the elves, too afraid to meet us face to face, preferring to kill us in our sleep, or kill our young and our females. An orc would rather give up and go home than lower himself to this sort of nonsense. That's why a wise *Khagan* will employ goblins where he can. You can get all the dirty work done without losing face, and you don't have to order any orcs to do anything they're not happy about. This is important when you have to keep your orcs in line and maintain a bit of order.

Some orcs don't have such a keen grip on the Harrowing as others, and you can ask them to do things other orcs are going to get uppity about, but mainly you'll want to use goblins. It's your job as *Khagan* to bring victory to your orcs, and that means making the battle easier any way you can. As long as you don't break the

14 Any form of combat that doesn't involve a full frontal assault is seen as 'low fighting' by the orcs, and therefore beneath them. Strength and mastery of arms will always earn more respect than tactics, guile, or misdirection.

spirit of the Harrowing personally, then you're still fit to lead.[15] Fighting within the spirit of the Harrowing is one thing, but getting orcs killed needlessly is another.

15 The orcs are quite brazen about this, and some even go so far as to say the goblins were created to do the jobs that orcs feel are beneath them. Maintaining the code of the Harrowing is intensely important to some orcs, although Kani always seemed rather ambivalent about it, often treating it as an obstacle to his rule.

3

TACTICS OF THE ORCS

The following talk was overheard when two Khagan from other tribes came to hear Kani Breakspeare's wisdom.[1] The Khagan had ventured from the Kourgaad Pass to hear the Ur-Khagan. They made much of the fact that Kani had been close to Asaan Firebringer and it was for this reason they travelled so far.

– V.

1 *Khagan* is the orc term for leader, the literal translation being 'Great One'. A *Khagan* leads a tribe which can consist of anything from ten to three hundred orcs. An *Ur-Khagan* is a 'Very Great One' and usually leads two or three tribes. His work is difficult due to the orcs' habit of 'scrapping', which is to test one's strength against another tribe. Beneath these titles is the rank of *Khagi*, which is an orc entrusted to lead a unit of troops. A *Khagan* usually has his own retinue, who are all referred to individually as *Khagi* too.

TACTICS OF ASAAN FIREBRINGER

Asaan Firebringer took the old myths seriously, not least the stories of orcs being born from the fires of the south. Before he united the tribes I thought he was going to become a shaman. I had even considered becoming one myself, but we both agreed being a *Khagan* was a far better thing. Asaan Firebringer took his name from the way he conducted his wars. Just like the great forest fires in the old myths, we orcs consume all in our path with hungry flames. When Asaan Firebringer became *Ur-Khagan* he took the time to teach his *Khagan* the five ways to attack: Burn, Consume, Confuse, Deplete, Destroy.

BURN

The most obvious way is to burn your enemy. Shoot him with arrows soaked in tar and lit from campfires. Use torches to burn his horses and set fire to his cloak. Throw oil over armoured men and watch them roast alive. Fire on the battlefield causes panic and horror. Elves and men have no stomach for war when they have to listen to the sounds of their kin being burnt alive. The smell of charred flesh unsettles the sturdiest opponent. Orcs on the other hand just start feeling hungry. Only the dwarves hold their ground, too proud to fall back and too slow to retreat.

Asaan also used to speak of burning not just in a literal sense, but in the way fuel is consumed. Let the enemy exhaust himself both in strength and casualties until he has nothing left. If he is stationary, then make him

advance a long distance, tiring his men. If he has great numbers, then thin him out with arrows and skirmishing attacks. This is how we burn our enemies – reduce his numbers and exhaust his troops.

CONSUME

The next way to attack with fire is to burn your opponent's supplies. This is a gamble for orcs, who depend not just on obtaining the weapons and armour of our enemies, but also on scavenging food. Burning supplies reduces enemy confidence and makes their leader act desperately. The next battle you fight will be so much easier if your opponent's supplies of arrows are set ablaze. The enemy will need to eat – armies do not feed themselves. Elves, dwarves and orcs will have trains of supplies to sustain them as they conduct war on the plains. Send off lightly armoured orcs to find the enemy's wagons and steal them. Those wagons you cannot steal must be burnt. Soldiers cannot fight when they are starving, and a general cannot easily form plans if he is thinking of his stomach.

CONFUSE

Try to burn your opponent's messengers whenever you can. Not literally, although that's good too. Tying an elf to a tree and setting fire to the whole thing is good for the orc spirit. However, you don't want just to burn the messenger, you must burn the entire way the enemy communicates. If the messengers don't deliver orders from the enemy leader, you can take advantage of the chaos. If messengers fail to report back, you can savour your opponent's uncertainty. Dispatching orcs to hunt messengers seems at odds with the spirit of Harrowing, but it is just a minor part of a bigger plan. It brings no dishonour to the *Khagan* that orders it, and in time will bring him victory. Goblins are best for this sort of work, and excel at sneaking around and ganging up on lone riders.

Deplete

During sieges or the sacking of towns you should raze the warehouses first. Target half of them and let the enemy busy himself trying to extinguish the fire. Every man, elf or dwarf carrying a pail of water is one less soldier aiming a bow or wielding a sword. If you have a good supply of food, then you can target every warehouse and watch the enemy's army descend into chaos. A siege can be reduced dramatically by spoiling or destroying the enemy's food.

Another type of warehouse is a stable. A stable is just a warehouse with horses in it. If you want to avoid facing heavy horse or mounted archers on the battlefield, then you should attack the stables. Elves will go to any lengths to rescue their horses. It is during this moment of panic that your troops can move with impunity.

Destroy

The last way to attack by fire is by burning your opponent's equipment. If dwarves own catapults and ballistae then you should act quickly. A small team of orcs with a good measure of pitch and a torch can ruin months' worth of construction, saving the lives of count-less orcs.

Burning bridges stops an enemy moving reinforcements quickly, or gives you extra time to set up your battle line. Windmills are also a strategic target for burning, and men will run themselves ragged trying to rescue such buildings. Successful destruction also helps starve your opponent in the following season; not that I advise fighting such protracted wars.

CONDITIONS FOR VICTORY

To attack with the five ways of fire requires certain conditions. Fortune smiles most during the driest summers. Take your tribe to the shelter of a mountain during the spring rains or go and trade with the other orcs at the Great Meets.[2] Fire will not be your friend in winter, unless the weather stays fine. Burning arrows will quickly die, enemies can beat flames out with handfuls of snow, or rain will drown your plans before they take hold. You are better off using small numbers in unexpected raids during winter.

The other condition you will need on your side is the wind. A gentle wind can stoke the flames, a strong wind

2 A Great Meet is a traditional location where orc tribes come together. Orcs shun towns and cities and the concept is entirely at odds with their nomadic lifestyle. A small population of orcs live at the Great Meet all year round, but they are 'tribe-less' and treated little better than goblins. The orc tribes trade items, buy supplies and sell slaves at a Great Meet. It is also a place where orcs can meet goblins, who give them news of the dwarves. Inter-tribal marriages occur at this time, although this aspect of orc culture is steeped in secrecy, which I am entirely grateful for.

can spread fire through a town or encampment with terrible speed. Never underestimate the primal fear of fire. All creatures have that fear, but some put a better face on it than others.

Never attack from downwind. Always have the wind at your back and the enemy in front. Fire is not your ally any more than an ambitious *Khagi* is.[3] Fire will turn on you and your orcs if you don't pay heed to it.

Don't go rushing in to attack if fire breaks out in an enemy town or camp and your opponent keeps calm. Wait for the flames to do their work; let them grow high and consume. Let the fire do your work for you and then attack. If the fire fails to catch and burn, then wait longer.

If the fire does catch, then give the order and get in there. Make sure your orcs get down the front as quick as you can, but make sure they don't get carried away. Nothing worse than one unit of orcs stealing stuff from a warehouse while another unit is burning it down. Orcs are still far too keen to kill their own and it's your job as *Khagan* to make sure they kill the enemy, not each other. Go through your plan properly with your *Khagi*, and make each of your *Khagi* bring a mate who can give a hand with the shouting, or take over if the *Khagi* gets himself dead. If a *Khagi*'s mate does a good job, then give him his own unit. Sometimes it's the *Khagi*'s mate that does the real work, so keep that in mind.

3 *Khagi* is the orc word for 'little leader'. These orcs typically lead a unit of around twenty warriors with a second, or 'mate'. The orcs that form the *Khagan*'s retinue are also referred to as *Khagi*. *Khagi* are chosen for their ability to stop orcs brawling with each other, which they do through intimidation, or brawling. It didn't make any sense to me, either.

ΤΑCΤΙCS OF ΤΗΕ BROKEN SPEAR

The following day, after the visiting Khagan *had departed, I asked Kani what his personal tactics were. This is what he told me.*

– V.

Every *Khagi*'s mate dreams of being a *Khagi*, just as every *Khagi* wants to be the *Khagan* leading his tribe. *Khagan* get into their heads they want to be *Ur-Khagan*, leading three or four tribes. Orcs like to dream big, but most times keeping things smaller is keeping things simpler. Orcs are driven by the simple urge to get in to a fight, steal some food and leave. This forms the basis for all orc warfare and underpins the main values of the Harrowing. However, this thinking is best suited for a single tribe attacking a farmstead. When orcs go to war, a *Khagan* needs to think bigger. Gathering more tribes is just the start.

The more tribes you have, the more food you need. The more food you need means you have to raid bigger farms. Before long you'll find yourself raiding other tribes, villages and even towns. The more raids you go on, the more arrows you need, and there'll be more fights over the spoils and who gets what looted armour. You can spend entire days just sorting things out and not doing any fighting, which is a sad old state of affairs. It makes your brains ache too. Attacking towns is hard work but there are ways of doing it without losing strength. No point taking five dozen orcs to a fight and only coming back with three dozen. That's when you start getting challengers come calling. Just because there are so many of us, don't mean an orc is expendable.

Except, of course, when you need to eat him.

STRENGTH IN NUMBERS

A good *Khagan* will attempt to outnumber his opponent four to one. This isn't as difficult as it sounds. It's easy to remember four to one, because there is one of you and four points worth remembering: Breed, Surround, Strike and Squabble.

BREED

Firstly, orcs breed faster than the other races. Well, maybe not as fast as humans – *they* spread like weeds. Orcs have more youngsters than dwarves and a lot more than elves. There are simply more of us, and because we don't live in cities no one really knows just how many of us there really are. There are tribes in the south I've never heard of, just as they've never heard of me. Well, they might have heard of me; I'm pretty bloody famous these days.

I'm sure there are orcs on the other side of the Bitterfang Mountains that have never been to one of the Great Meets I've been to. And there are plenty of us down south, still living in the Diresand Desert, getting their brains baked out by the sun. There are bloody loads of us and we're everywhere, and it's because the Harrowing is so strict on not killing females and young 'uns.

Secondly, you've got to use scouts. Some orcs have issued challenges to me, saying using scouts isn't in the spirit of Harrowing. I say, if you know where the enemy is, then you can surround him easier and cut off his escape route. You want to give him just enough hope that he doesn't think he's about to fight a last stand. Humans couldn't fight a last stand if their lives depended on it.[4] Elves get all maudlin and will often fight in such a way that some give their lives to make sure others escape. These elves run back to the forests and get more elves, who come looking for trouble. Never, ever, make a dwarf think he's fighting a last stand. It's like shouting at the sea and expecting the tide not to come in. It's like having an argument with a stone. An argument you'll lose every time. Dwarves will go berserker on you, shouting about how their fathers' fathers are watching from the Great Hall. I hate it when they get like this.

STRIKE

The other thing about using scouts is that you'll know how many of the enemy there are, which helps when it comes to outnumbering him four to one. Make sure your scouts can count, though, otherwise you'll come unstuck. A goblin reporting that there are 'a lot of elves on horses'

4 I'm fairly certain this witticism was unintentional, but it was difficult to know with Kani; he seemed to have a witty streak that was entirely out of place with the orc character.

is not helpful. Scouts will tell you where the enemy is, so you can show up somewhere else if you can't outnumber them. 'Attack where the enemy ain't' is what Asaan Firebringer said.[5] Raiding unprotected farms and supplies is my favourite way to wage war. Maximum profit for minimum dead. That's the plan of a wise *Khagan*. You've got yourself a real problem when orcs start turning up dead in their dozens. No one likes to lose, orcs especially. Some of the tribe will whine on about not having a good fight afterwards, so you'll have to encourage them to have a good brawl to get all that fury out of their system.

SQUABBLE

Lastly, you need the odds stacked in your favour, because at any given time about a quarter of your army will be squabbling and brawling with each other. Orcs argue among themselves. It don't matter how stern the *Khagi* or how impressive the *Khagan*, orcs are going to fall out and fight. They might be hungry; they might have divided the spoils badly last battle; they might just be hungover. Orcs don't really need a reason to start a brawl with each other – it's part of our nature. I've lost count of the number of times a well-planned raid or battle has gone up in flames due to a *Khagi* losing control of his

5 'Attack where the enemy ain't' is deeply unpopular with orcs, who settle in to a kind of depression if they feel they have missed an opportunity to kill something. At times like these some of the orcs were too depressed to even pick fights with each other, which I was profoundly grateful for.

unit and not being able to carry out orders, which brings me to discipline.[6]

khagi, khagan, ur-khagan and the power of influence

A *Khagi* is possibly the most important orc on the battlefield. As soon as you lose the *Khagi* you don't have an army any more, you just have a rabble with weapons. A *Khagan* should spend time with his *Khagi* and tell them wise stuff and where they're going wrong. When you spend time with a *Khagi* the orcs in his unit think he's got the *Khagan*'s favour. Everyone wants to be a noticed by the *Khagan*, so when you speak with one of your *Khagi* it adds to his prestige, which means the orcs in that unit are less likely to brawl with each other.

Another way you can do this is to swap members of your own retinue for the *Khagi* leading the more troublesome units. The orcs in those units will feel like the *Khagan* is keeping his eye on them. They'll try to keep their mind on the battle and look impressive. As soon as a unit feel like the *Khagan* isn't watching them they'll kick off, starting trouble among themselves or, worse yet, with other units.[7] You need give attention to all your *Khagi*, even the ones that make you want to kick them in

6 'Gone up in flames' is an idiom that orcs and humans share. The idiom may have originated with the orcs, or it may just be a coincidence of language that both races invented it and kept it in use.

7 This makes orc warriors sound like naughty school children, which they are, if those children were five and half feet tall, armed, bloodthirsty lunatics with scant regard for their own lives.

the arse each day. Especially those ones. These are the ones that will get ahead of themselves and challenge you when you've got two dozen other things to sort out.

As *Ur-Khagan* you have to make sure that the *Khagan* who answer to you all feel equal, otherwise there'll be tension among the tribes and that's the last thing you want. There's always going to be an element of rivalry, but you need to be sure it doesn't spill over into open hostility. I've had to declare days of open brawling before a major battle, just so all the orcs could get the bad blood out of their system.[8] Make sure all the weapons are put away first, just in case anyone gets tempted to take things too far. Fortunately orcs don't hold on to grudges like dwarves do. It's doubtful we'd ever get anything done if we did.

---

8 A day of brawling allows two tribes to vent their displeasure on each other without any casualties, mostly. This *Ur-Khagan*-sanctioned inter-tribe brawling is called a 'mosh' in the orc tongue. Some orcs only participate for the first hour or two, then leave. This is called 'mosh and go' and frowned upon heavily by right-minded orcs.

4

BLADES AND BASHERS

The following chapter is a translation of the conversation I had with Kani Breakspeare, Ur-Khagan of the Scarsfaalen Tribes, as he inspected a cache of weapons.

– V.

KNIVES

Every orc carries a knife – two if he wants to last the year, three if he has any ambition. An orc mother's main duty is to make sure her offspring has enough to eat and that they get a knife when they're five summers old. Don't really matter too much where it's from. Dwarf knife. Elf knife. Human knife. All the same when you get down to it. Better than flint, which is all we had for a long time. Some of our kin know how to make knives now, but it takes a long time. Better to take them from defeated enemies and give them to the next generation of orcs.

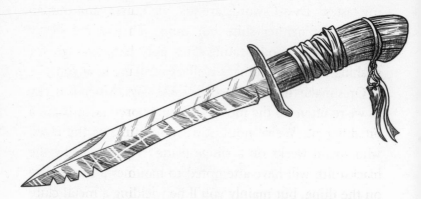

Mainly we use knives as tools, but they can also be good for discouraging orcs who are getting a bit rowdy. 'A little stab in the leg never hurt no one' – that's what the previous *Ur-Khagan* said.[1] Still, he was often so drunk you could shoot him in the arse with a crossbow and he wouldn't notice until the following morning, but that's orcs for you.

SWORDS

Swords are harder to come by. Elves get right uppity when they drop their swords. Part of me thinks *quick, strike while they're unarmed*, and another part of me thinks they're less dangerous when they *do* have their swords.

1 This is worryingly true. Orcs don't get upset about stabbing the same way humans do. Sometimes they even stab each other for fun. I suspect orc blood clots more quickly than human blood and the propensity to bleed to death is reduced significantly. It may be these random stabbings toughen up orc skin for future attacks. Most orcs do seem to be covered in scar tissue, happily sporting open wounds that would become infected if left untreated in a human.

Stealing elf swords is hard work and they're a little light for my tastes.[2] Dwarf swords are just big knives, and human swords are neither shite nor dung. They're not heavy enough for a good beating, and not sharp enough for slashing. A bit like humans really, sod all use to anyone.

Orcs make their own swords these days, which is tricky as we're often on the move. Of course orcs' swords are a bit different. We've not got as much time as the elves, who spend weeks on a single blade. If you're lucky the blacksmith will have attempted to hammer a sharp edge on the thing, but mainly you'll be wielding a metal club. Most swords are made at the Great Meets, often by human slaves. These ones seem to have more of an edge, probably because the human making it doesn't want a kicking from his owner.[3]

Some like to think orcs are weaker than humans just because we're a handspan shorter.[4] However, orcs are

2 I did try and explain to Kani that the *aelfir* are more interested in a sharp edge than a heavy blade. This earned me a stern look and the none-too-gentle warning that if I was going to get 'funny ideas' I could 'sod off and live in the bloody forest'.

3 There are a surprising number of human slaves at the Great Meets. I sensed that human craftsmen were sought after despite Kani's continued complaint they were only good for eating. Many were the times a *Khagan* offered a selection of goods to buy me, which only added to my anxiety.

4 Many war stories are in fact tall stories, especially when the orcs involved are over seven feet tall. This is rare in the extreme as most pureblood orcs are bow-legged and slightly stooped. They rarely reach anything over five and half feet tall. Some orcs, including Kani Breakspeare himself, claim to be of mixed blood. These orcs are usually taller and stronger than their kin on account of having trolls featuring in their lineage.

always on the move, always fighting. We build muscle differently from humans, and plenty different from elves. Humans are lazy too, always wanting to do boring stuff like farming or building houses. Elves are little better and sit around singing to trees and other nonsense. That's why we have such prodigious strength, and that's why we will always have the advantage in close-quarters combat.

It's this strength that makes it difficult to parry strikes from orcs with swords. Humans nearly always buckle and often find themselves disarmed. Dwarves have the tenacity and strength to meet our attacks and turn them aside. Elves are much simpler: you either hit them or you don't. If they fail to move out of the way, they're as good as dead.

'If you can't break his face, break his arms' is a popular saying among orcs that like using swords. Once an opponent has a broken shoulder he can't parry or make counter-attacks. Once his legs are broken he can't run away. Fighting with a sword is simply a case of wearing your opponent down until he runs out of limbs. Then you're able to smash his brains out while he flops about on the ground like a landed fish.

AXES

I bloody love an axe.[5] You know where you are with an axe. All that force of the downswing is focused in to one

5 He really does. He has a cart loaded with axes and knows where he stole each one from and whom he had to kill to plunder it. It takes a very long time to tell all of those stories I can tell you, especially when the narrator insists you write them all down. And becomes increasingly drunk as he does so.

narrow leading edge. An axe is proper good for smashing in dwarf heads, especially as you need an axe to get past the armour. Dwarves rarely go anywhere without a steel hat on. Nothing quite mashes up a shield like an axe, which is another good reason to carry them.

Elves also wear armour and have sturdy breastplates too. Giving an elf a good wallop will shatter their little pansy ribs. You don't even need to puncture the metal, just smash them in the chest. Once you've broken an elf's ribs he'll struggle to draw breath, which is a shame because I like to hear him scream before I take his head off. Taking an enemy's head off is the whole point of a good axe. Even a scrawny elf neck puts up a bit of resistance when you're hacking it. Cutting an orc head off can take a dozen strikes, but you'll want to go for one clean, solid cut, especially if you're facing off against a challenger.

It doesn't occur to most orcs that you can parry with an axe. It's not easy and it takes a lot of practice. Parrying with a one-handed axe isn't so much fun but you should have a shield, so use that instead. Parrying with a two-handed axe is easier and you might find an opportunity to disarm your opponent during the same exchange.

The best axes are made by the dwarves; they may not be able to run fast but they do know how to make an axe head. The first thing any half-sensible orc will do when he's looted a dwarf axe is to get rid of the shaft. Much better to have a longer handle made of the heaviest wood you can find. I always get a spare handle made, but I'm strange like that, always thinking about the future. That's probably why they made me *Ur-Khagan*.[6]

Humans use axes too, although they're nearly as fascinated with swords as the elves are, giving them silly names and all sorts. If you can't get a dwarf axe then get a human one. Elf axes are as rare as red rain.[7] Orc-made axes are durable, rather than sharp, but at least come with a sensible haft that can be used one or two-handed.

6 Although this sounds unlikely, it is true. Many orcs in the Scarsfaalen tribes wanted an *Ur-Khagan* who was as intelligent as the mysterious shamans. The shamans gathered a great deal of influence during the leadership of Asaan Firebringer, but were rumoured to have their own agenda.

7 'Rare as red rain' is a common expression among orcs. Asaan Firebringer often promised the sky would rain blood after every non-orc on the face of Near Evain had been exterminated. Many orcs grew disillusioned after Asaan Firebringer was killed at the battle of Fuendil's End, pouring scorn on his promises. As rare as red rain is a perfect example of the orcs' sense of disappointment.

HAMMERS

Hammers are a bit like swords only more fun. In fact they're so much fun they're nearly axes, but that's another weapon entirely. Hammers are good for most things – breaking bones or denting armour. They also smash up elf longbows nicely too, which is handy in the middle of the fighting, but not so handy if you want to loot them afterwards.

A one-handed hammer used with a shield is a nice bit of gear for an orc to march to war with. An orc with a two-handed hammer will need to put himself in the middle of the battle line to make sure he gets down the front, else there's no point in him turning up. Some orcs like to call a two-handed hammer 'a warhammer', but I think warhammer is a bloody stupid name. Course it's a warhammer; orcs don't use them to make barns, do they?

SPEAR

We used these to hunt boar. Still do when we can get into a forest, which isn't often because the elves get all uppity. I bloody love a bit of boar. Well, half a boar. Anything less is just something to snack on between meals. Slow roasted for preference.

Anyway, spears.

At first we'd use bit of stick with a sharp stone tied to it. Then the elves started sticking swords on the end of shafts and bringing them to battle. We thought that was

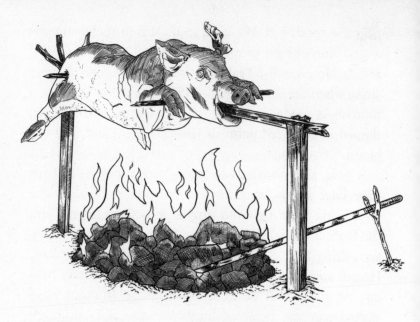

pretty stupid.[8] What we did notice, though, was arrows. Spear is just a big arrow, right? It's good for all sorts. Good against soldiers on foot, really good against heavy horses, good against soldiers with swords. You can throw it too, but that's not such a great idea. All you've got then is three knives and sod all chance of leaving the battle field alive. Of course, dwarf spears are no use to no one. They're too big to be arrows and too small to be spears. I hate fighting dwarves. Unless they've got axes I can loot afterwards. The best people to steal spears from are humans. Humans are less dangerous than dwarves and make surprisingly good spears.

It's quite fashionable to tie a red flourish to the shaft

8 The orcs often talk of the stupidity of the elves, of their preoccupation with unnecessary decoration, the time they waste with ceremonies, and the ridiculous weapons they use, all except the elf longbow.

near the spearhead. We used to do this to make aurochs angry. Aurochs get proper uppity when they see a bit of red. In time we also realised it's harder to parry a spear strike when the shaft has a flourish attached to it. A good flourish is made out of wool and tightly woven, then dipped in good red paint. If you can't get paint, just use blood.

A wise *Khagan* needs to make sure about half of his tribe have spears, and always when facing cavalry. The elves bring their high and mighty to war on horses, and the high and mighty can't resist rushing over and doing something heroic. That's when you get the spear out. Horses aren't too keen on charging a wall of spikes held out on seven-foot poles. Unfortunately, humans have started copying the elves' heavy horse tactics. Although not as skilled on horseback, humans still do a lot of damage to an unprepared unit of orcs. If the unit don't have spears, you can assume they won't survive, and if they do they'll fall back. This isn't cowardice; being charged by heavy horse ain't fun.

Lately I've been encouraging the blacksmiths to make spears with three jags on the back of the blade. You've got to thrust in deep with this, but when you pull it out the jags catch and pull out your opponent's guts. Not much use against someone in a breastplate, but surprisingly good against an unprotected horse belly. A horse won't go too far with its guts hanging out, and if you're lucky the mount will crush the rider as it falls. Sometimes the rider will just get his leg broke, but that's fun too. If you're unlucky the horse will crush you as it falls, so stay awake and be ready to get out of the way. After the battle

45

is done you cook the horses. They're all right. Not as good as boar, mind.

Some *Khagan* will try to give his whole tribe spears, which is admirable but not always the right choice. Sometimes it's better to give an orc a spare spear, especially if he's right down the front,[9] although you'll want to think about your flanks too. Spears break easily, especially when you're fending off heavy horse. The enemy leader will think a unit of spears will be useless after being charged by heavy horse and charge them again. That's when you get the spare spears out and give them a surprise. All of a sudden those orcs don't look so stupid any more, eh?

MAUL

Thing I love about the maul, even more than an axe (and I bloody love an axe), is that they're cheap, and even an idiot can make one. This is a good thing when you're trying to lead a tribe of orcs. It's not that orcs are stupid, far from it, but they do get bored easily. Spending weeks making one sword is not really in the orc character, so you need to find something that can be made quickly.

The maul is like half a spear shaft. Or maybe a third of one if you're desperate. I've seen smaller ones but they look daft. So, you've got your shaft, and you make a hole

---

9 Kani Breakspeare often spoke of being 'down the front', meaning at the vanguard. 'Down the front' is a source of great pride to all orcs. Often times not being 'down the front' is akin to not having taken part in the battle at all. When Kani spoke of 'being down the front' he would be overtaken by a deep wistfulness that I had not expected to see among the orcs.

for the spike. The spike is made from steel and it's cone-shaped, see, like from a fir tree. Part of the metal extends from each side of the wood. I like a long spike for reasons I'm coming to. You've got two options with a maul: you can use the flat bit like a hammer; or you can use the spike on the other side like a, well, like a spike really.

Remember what I was saying about axes focusing force to a narrow edge? Well, the maul does that twenty times better. All that muscle, sinew, downforce and bad language gets brought to a steel point. Dwarf armour, elf armour, human armour – it all gets busted up bad when you've got a maul in your hands. The point forces through and you leave your opponent with a nice deep puncture wound. You can't fight if you can't breathe and people flop around like fishes when they have holes punched in them. I always strike at the sides of an opponent, as the armour is thinner there.

The other option with the maul is to use it like a hammer. You can't fight properly if your brains are scrambled, and you can't hear orders from your leader if your ears are ringing. A helmet is like a big bell, so make sure you hammer on it and make it ring. You can also use the flat side of a maul to bust up a shield. Opponents get pretty downhearted when they see their shield get wrecked, so use this to your advantage and keep pressing the attack.

You can use a small maul one-handed, which gives you the option of a shield. That's good for lots of orcs, but I always preferred a two-handed maul, especially since I nicked that human breastplate and had it fixed. Even if a *Khagan* doesn't have access to a lot of steel you can still equip a lot of orcs. The best thing to do when things get bad is to melt down human swords and make maul heads. You might get as many as five mauls out of one human sword, which is far better.

The other thing a good *Khagan* will do is make sure his archers have got a one-handed maul hanging from their belt. Our bows don't have the range of other races and orc archers are just as likely to end up down the front as everyone else. Giving an archer a maul makes him useful, is what I always say.

khukri or kingslayer

While not a popular weapon, there are a few dozen orcs who are keen to use a pair of matched khukri. These orcs usually fancy themselves as proper ferocious, banging on that they could be berserkers. Stupid arses mainly. The blade features a heavy, angled section that allows the blade to fall faster and with more force than a traditional knife. This weighted weapon is perfect for frenzied hacking, and well suited for orcs. A single khukri can be used for slashing and stabbing attacks and can be used to parry too. When used as a pair they present an intimidating opponent surrounded by flashing steel. It takes a while to learn how to fight with a weapon in both hands.

A lot of orcs don't have the grace for it. There's plenty of orcs who have lost a limb when their ambition exceeded their coordination.

Most khukri are around a foot long, but Asaan Firebringer wielded a pair about a foot and half long on account of his size.[10] The handles are made of hardwood or horn and they're cheaper to make than swords due to the shorter blade. For many orcs, including me, the weapon is a symbol of when our greatest victory was taken from us. The weapon was dubbed Kingslayer after the Battle of Salt Wind when Asaan Firebringer killed the elven High King.[11] It was in this moment of savage triumph that the bravest of all *Ur-Khagan* dropped his guard. It was then that an avenging elf bodyguard struck, and it was then the Asaanic Wars came to an end.

LONGBOW

I've never really understood the bow. I can see the use of it, but the simple matter is that orc bows are never going to be elf bows. Orc archers mean well – they keep talking

10 Orc folk tales variously report that Asaan Firebringer was anything from six to eight feet tall. They also state he could give an enemy the evil eye, never slept, rarely washed, and had intercourse with three females a day. I couldn't help but be reminded of King Arendsonn.

11 The Battle of Salt Wind is known as Fuendil's End to the *aelfir* and the humans of Hoim. The *aelfir* have turned the events of this titanic battle in to an epic song. Salt Wind has since passed into orc idiom as being a byword for disappointment. For example: 'It'll be a salt wind that blows if we don't get more supplies soon.'

about the future of warfare – but I'm buggered if it makes much difference on the battlefield.

Like the sword, this is simply a matter of construction. Elves know more about wood than any other race, so it stands to reason they know how to make superior long-bows. Our longbows break too often for my taste and the archers are always complaining about how their strings aren't good enough.

Then there's the matter of honour. No archer can honestly say he really wants to get down the front. What's the point of going to battle if you're not going to smash some dwarf's head in, or break an elf's legs just to hear them squeal? Orcs who do fight at close quarters are going to be reluctant to share the spoils with any orcs that don't. This is going to cause friction, so keep on your guard at the battle's end.

Longbows do have some uses. Enemy light cavalry can be cut down by a solid volley of arrows. A charge from heavy horse won't stall, but it will be distracted, possibly enough to make a vital mistake. I've seen elves pulled off their horses because they were more worried about the arrows bouncing off their shields than the soldiers they were charging.

The advantage longbows have over crossbows is that they can fire up and over.[12] I tell the orcs in front of the archers to wear their shields on their backs and keep their

12 'Up and over', or an indirect volley of arrows, is not a popular tactic among orcs, particularly the orcs in front of the archers. Orc archers can escape injury for an entire battle, only to receive 'a good kicking' after the battle from their own comrades for a perceived or real injury caused by an accidental shooting.

heads down. Elves use this tactic on us all the time, so I quite like returning the insult.[13] Elves, like dwarves, won't run away, but they might suffer a few wounded. Humans get proper anxious and just look for an excuse to sod off. Longbow arrows give them plenty of incentive.

Lastly, and this ain't a popular thing to say to orcs, is the fact that our eyesight isn't as good as other races. We're better at night, but during the day the brightness causes a few problems. This fact also stands against orcs mastering the longbow. There's plenty of times an orc has been killed by an elf before he even knew the elf was there.

CROSSBOW

Humans are good for five things: raising crops; running away; shitting their pants; making spears; and, perhaps best of all, making crossbows. The only thing better than a human crossbow is a dwarf one, but getting hold of them is like trying to pull teeth from a wolf.

The crossbow is slower to fire than the longbow and has a shorter range, but it does cut through armour. The bolts are smaller than arrows and orc blacksmiths have mastered making them, a fact which continually pleases and surprises me. Some crossbows have little handles to

13 'Returning the insult' is a turn of phrase comparable to the human expression 'returning the compliment', except orcs don't really have any compliments. Orc insults range from outright challenges to light-hearted cussing that can mean anything from 'Good morning' to 'I see you've copulated with your mother. Again.'

winch the string back, others have big levers. A *Khagan* will need to put a crossbow in the hands of an orc who is strong enough to reload it (which is all of us), smart enough to fix it (that narrows things down a bit) and can see clearly further than sixty feet (also tricky). This sort of orc is rare, so look after them.

Anyone with heavy armour on will think twice about approaching a unit with crossbows. Heavy horse charges come unstuck, swordsmen get cut down, and anyone who isn't carrying a shield will have a very bad day. Suffice to say, I really like crossbows – I even have one myself, but I rarely get a chance to use it on account of being down the front so often.

The essence of the crossbow is in the timing. You need to be ready to fire as soon as the enemy is in range. As soon as the unit has fired, you must reload and fire again. The first volley will only soften up the enemy. The second volley will devastate them on account of the fact they're much closer. Failure to guess the range correctly on the first volley is bloody stupid; failure to reload in time for a second volley is unforgivable. Make sure you appoint an orc with good eyesight to lead your crossbow unit. Then make sure everyone else listens to him. Losing a unit of crossbows is a harsh blow to an orc army, but losing the battle and not being able to retrieve the weapons afterwards is worse still.

Even though orcs armed with crossbows can enjoy disproportionate success they are still not down the front. You'll need to be hard and fair when the spoils are divided up, or you'll have the same problem I mentioned earlier about archers.

the scavenger spirit

Orcs endure and survive, but they also learn how to use the weapons of their enemies whenever they can. Attacking your opponent with a weapon made by one of his kin will fill him with fury. It might just fill him with fear too. If he runs away, then you can laugh your arse off. If he gets mad, then you've got yourself a good fight, so get stuck in. Whatever happens, you must always, always retrieve weapons and armour from the fallen. Even if you've no use for the weapon you may be able to reforge it into something useful. Like an axe.

5

AN ORC'S GUIDE TO ARMOUR

It was following a small raid on a farmstead in the Arendsonn Kingdom that Kani Breakspeare decided to enlighten me on the orc attitude to armour. What follows is a transcript of that conversation.

– V.

THE SUBTLE ART OF INTIMIDATION

It's a salt wind that blows on an orc what don't have his own armour. Oftentimes it's armour what gives an orc a bit of confidence. You need that when you're marching off to cause trouble. No one wants to get down the front without some protection on them. Still, many orcs miss the point with armour.

No warrior should enter combat thinking he's completely invincible. Armour has weak points, joints and so on. Leather armour might stop the worst from a sword's slash, but it's of little use against hammer blows. A helmet will deflect an arrow, but it won't stop an axe mashing your brains in. If someone covers you in oil you'll burn just the same, armoured up or not. And if you find yourself in deep water with a breastplate on you'll drown in minutes.[1]

Good armour provides a measure of protection, but also makes the wearer appear more fearsome. Being fearsome isn't a problem orcs struggle with much, but it's all to the good if you look proper terrifying. Most orcs complain when I say this, but if your opponent runs away without putting up a fight, then that's one less enemy to worry about. The enemy aren't going to worry too much if a dozen orcs turn up to fight wearing nothing but leather britches.[2] But if those same twelve orcs arrive wearing leather cuirasses and are armed with shields, well, that's a different matter. Add in a banner with a couple of decapitated heads, decorate them with plenty of horns and tusks, and suddenly those dozen orcs are an ugly proposition.[3]

Wearing heavier armour is at odds with the orcs' raiding tactics. It's only during the most bitter battles that rank and file orcs should consider getting a

1 Orcs hate water almost as much as they hate elves. Water is at odds with the orc character both in terms of their creation myths and the terrible stench they revel in. It is perhaps unsurprising that orcs are poor swimmers, despite their strength.

2 I disagree. I for one would worry if twelve half-dressed orcs arrived to fight, but not as much as twelve naked orcs, who would almost certainly be berserkers.

3 As if orcs could be anything other than an ugly proposition.

breastplate on. Orcs tend to keep their protection light and stay mobile where possible. We're a nomadic people and there's very little difference between our everyday lives and the days we raid. War is a different matter, but wearing a breastplate and walking dozens of miles is not going to do you any favours.

Apart from give you really strong legs.

ꝼeꞇishes

Orcs tend to decorate their armour with animal teeth. Elf teeth and human teeth are tiny and look ridiculous, and dwarf teeth ain't much better. Some orcs go as far as to wear bones, even using skulls to decorate their shoulder guards. I've always thought this was an invitation for trouble. When bone shatters it breaks off sharp, and I've always had a healthy respect for sharp things coming near my face. It's like I always say, 'You've got two eyes;

look after them and they'll keep looking for you.' I'm all in favour of decorating armour so orcs look terrifying, but only so long as it doesn't stop them fighting. Being injured by your own armour makes you a laughing stock too.

The shamans have got wise to orc desire to decorate their armour. They sell trinkets and fetishes to any orc gullible enough to part with something valuable. Lucky wolf fangs, raven feathers of quickness, auroch bollocks (for bravery, obviously) and pet toads. What a load of old guff. Still, if it makes the orc wearing it a bit surlier, or more ferocious, I'm all in favour. And all that weirdness scares the dung out of humans, which is no bad thing.

LEATHER ARMOUR

Leather armour is the absolute mainstay of all orcs. Most orcs will happily sleep in leather armour.[4] Some veterans don't even bother taking it off to wash themselves. Good leather armour is boiled to make the leather harder. There was a fashion among orcs to boil the leather in wax. That idea was quickly shunned when they discovered sharp swords, particularly elf swords, cut through it too easily. These days most orcs just boil the leather as it is, then spend the first couple of months

4 Something I learned to do after a month's worth of sleepless nights. Sleeping in armour on the bare ground is a unique torture that no learned man should ever be forced to endure. This, combined with the lack of soap, cutlery, available tea and well-mannered games of chance, nearly cost me my sanity.

pissing on it. I don't know why.[5] Perhaps it's something to do with marking one's territory, or gear in this case.

Most orcs will have a leather tunic at the very least. Many feature a number of straps that fall vertically to the knee, like a skirt. I've always thought these were a bit useless, but an orc in a skirt is a proper terrible sight. Leather bracers are also very popular, as are gauntlets. A fairly wealthy orc will also get himself some trousers made up too. Some orcs have even had little hats made,

5 The fact that some orcs smell worse than they look is a revelation I've still yet to come to terms with. Perhaps most shocking at all is that orc females actually seem to be attracted to the more pungent-smelling members of the tribe. Some nights I awaken from a nightmare and could swear the smell of orc urine haunts my chamber.

but I think they're uncomfortable on the ears. Bear in mind that leather armour won't help you in the slightest against dwarves and their hammers.

ΤΗΕ GREATCOAT

In winter time an orc might wear a greatcoat if he can afford it.[6] No *Khagan* should be without one as he always needs to look proper impressive. This leather garment

6 The orc greatcoat goes by a variety of names, the most popular being Mahk Intozche. Mahk meaning 'rain' and Intozche meaning 'go away before I give you a kicking'. This provides a perfect example of how the orc language itself is particularly aggressive, even when elements such as weather are the subject.

reaches an orc's knees. The right side fastens across the whole chest by means of a button by the left armpit, the coat effectively doubles its thickness this way. Some orcs even stitch rings of metal to the front or shoulders of their coat. The price you pay in additional weight is more than justified when you consider how intimidating an armoured coat looks. The lining is wolf fur, which is bloody difficult to get hold of on account of having to kill the bastard things. The fur does keep you warm in winter, though. The coat is gathered at the waist by a thick leather belt, which acts as a point to hang a sword or club from.

All these items are usually made at the Great Meets and don't need to be stolen from other races, which is just as well. Orcs are broader across the shoulder and more barrel-chested than other creatures. Stealing armour from elves is pointless as it's much too small; dwarf armour might be good for goblins, but only fat bastards. Human armour can be modified a bit, but often needs a lot of work.

bReAsTpLaTes

Much like the weapons we use, breastplates are best stolen from the enemy and customised to fit the new wearer. Dwarf breastplates are best, although they do tend to leave the midriff exposed. I like to wear elf chain underneath my breastplate, but don't tell anyone or they'll think I've gone soft.

A breastplate also tells you a bit about an orc, in addition to providing protection. He must have earned the right to wear it, otherwise the *Khagan* would have

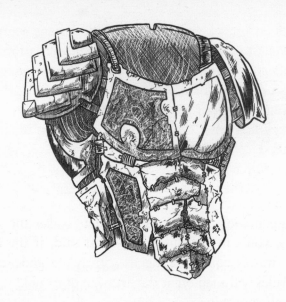

had it off him when the spoils were divided up. He must be rich too, in order to pay someone to alter it for him. An orc in a breastplate is most likely a *Khagi* of the *Khagan*'s retinue, or a veteran *Khagi* leading an old unit with a proper reputation. Either way, the breastplate tells other orcs loud and clear that the wearer is a big deal in the tribe, he can take a kicking, and, more importantly, he knows how to give a kicking. Awarding a breastplate to a *Khagi* is a good way of adding to his prestige and keeping him on your side. His unit will get a bit more serious about raiding and might even stop fighting each other.

CLAW BRACER

This is a weapon really, but it always gets stored with the armour. A claw bracer is a couple of curving knives welded to a metal bracer. This appeals to a lot of orcs

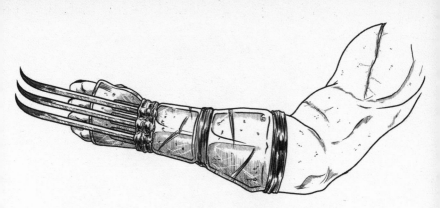

because it looks proper fierce. There's also the added bonus: you can't be disarmed. That said, if the blacksmith wasn't concentrating then there's a good chance the blades will snap off at the first sign of trouble. Typical orc craftsmanship.

You'll suffer a disadvantage of reach with every opponent you come up against. Don't matter if they've got sword, spear, hammer or maul. The claw bracer is a weapon for orcs that don't mind getting in close. Proper close. I tend to think of them as a backup weapon. Let the enemy think he's disarmed you, then give him a good stab in the guts. Of course, it's quite difficult to hide a couple of foot-long blades, so it won't be much of a surprise unless your opponent is an idiot. Like humans, for example.

Some orcs get metal shoulder guards made up that also have blades attached; knee guards too. I'm in two minds about this. I've seen veterans skewering their own brains because they thought a spike on their shoulder would make them look more ferocious. Ain't too much ferocious about a dead orc, especially if it's his own armour what kills him.

helmets

I hate helmets. They make your ears hurt and you can't hear a sodding thing. In summer they get so hot your brains feel like they're on the boil. Just about every orc I know feels the same way. And because orcs do so much fighting during the summer they're not widely used. The other problem is shape. Orc heads are a bit wider than other races and our necks are quite a bit shorter. Helmets just don't sit right on us, and that means we have to make them ourselves, which also counts against them.

There is one exception that makes a helmet worth wearing. Firstly, you'll want to get a helmet that leaves the face open. No point fighting if you can't see your opponent, and it's no fun if you can't shout at people when you're killing them. Shouting is the best bit of a good fight. Once you got a good open-faced helmet, you'll want to get some great big horns to stick on it. I like auroch horns best.[7] Just surround one of them with the tribe and make a circle like you do for a challenge. Then you need to avoid getting gored on those horns I mentioned. I punched my auroch into submission, but I understand *Khagan* that might want to use a weapon or something. Some orcs like deer antlers, but that's shite by comparison. I'd expect it from elves, never from orcs.

shields

A shield is a very important piece of kit for an orc. It's disposable, but completely necessary. We rely on shields the same way dwarves rely on heavy armour. Part of the reason is to defend against arrows. Many of our battles are fought against elves and humans who are obsessed with fighting at a distance. While a shield can't be depended on to save your life every time, it will improve your chances. No *Khagan* worth his salt goes anywhere without a wagon filled with spare shields.[8]

We make our shields from wicker on account of the

7 Huge, surly cattle that roam the Kourgaad Plains. Auroch feature heavily in orc life. Their skins are made into armour, orc young drink the milk, the blood is used to paint banners, the meat is eaten by all. The horns end up being used for everything from knife handles to short bows to helmet decoration.

8 Another reminder of how important salt is in orc culture. 'Worth his salt' or 'worth his weight in salt' might be equated to the Hoim expression 'worth his weight in gold'. Orcs have little use for gold, but use salt to cure auroch meat, in their cooking, and to ward off evil spirits. Orcs often rub their palms in salt before a battle to soak up sweat, improving their grip. 'Worth his salt' is not to be confused with 'a salt wind that blows', which is a negative expression.

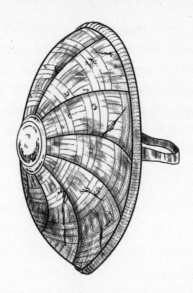

elves getting so uppity when we venture into the forests. You'll need to find a riverbank that's overgrown with reeds, or a few willow trees. The materials are made into a domed spiral of wicker, with a metal plate at the centre. The curve of the wicker dome is stronger than a flat surface made of the same material, standing up to more punishment in close quarters combat. The curving surface also deflects arrows unless the tip strikes the wicker straight on. Many orcs tar the inside of the shield and stick a circle of canvas in there. This gives the wicker something else to stick to. Weaving shields out of wicker takes a long time and is proper boring, but fortunately the female orcs do it on account of it being weaving.[9]

9 Orcs have very defined ideas about which sex performs which jobs. This isn't as straightforward as one might think. Orc butchers are female, as are weavers and often shaman. Orc females also fight, but are regarded with suspicion, although I suspect this is because orc males are wary of being shown up by the females.

We hold our shields differently from other races too. An elf or a human shield runs along the arm that bears it, but our shields are an extension of our fist. You can use the shield to punch your opponent, smashing his ribs, or striking his face. This type of attack is hard to parry. I've seen orcs smash the weapons from their opponents' hands in this way. Many units of orcs train specifically to push their opponents over. You just grab hold of the shield, get your head down, and run like your arse is on fire. This tactic is commonly known as a shield mauling. There's a good chance you'll knock your opponent down on account of the orc's prodigious strength. It's best to aim for the chest or shoulders if you're aiming at all. Don't try for the face or your opponent will just stab you in the guts as you draw near. Elves in particular go down fairly easy. Dwarves seem to be welded to the ground, so don't expect to upend one; just hope to break his nose. Once your opponent has lost his footing you can start hacking his limbs off. He'll be hard-pressed to defend himself.

Should the wicker come unravelled you'll still have the metal centre. Humans have something similar to this called a buckler. I'm no fan of the buckler, but I've been told it's quite satisfying to punch people with.[10] At the very least you can use it to punch aside sword blows and turn aside the odd strike. Better to have a little metal shield than no shield at all.

---

10 Note the continuous preoccupation with turning a defensive tool into something you can use to hurt an opponent. This is not unusual in any aspect of the orc psyche. Any mundane object's ultimate worth can be decided with the simple question, 'Yeah, but can you kill someone with it?' There is nothing the orc would immediately dismiss as a tool of potential destruction.

Lastly, the shield is useful during wet weather. Due to the conical shape, the shield can be worn as a hat.[11] This is another reason for sticking canvas or animal skin inside, otherwise the thing will leak. This is considerably more fun than carrying the thing, or slinging it over your back. While a shield is not heavy, it's always best to have your hands as free as possible when travelling.

11 An orc wearing his greatcoat and conical shield as a hat is an intimidating sight. Most rumours of 'civilised orcs' stem from an ignorant human seeing an orc attired in this way. I myself acquired an orc greatcoat which I have donated to the University of Hoim's cultural studies department.

6

AN ORC'S GUIDE TO TERRAIN

It was late autumn when we took shelter in the shadows of the Bitterfang Mountains, and it was then that Kani Breakspeare gave another of his long lectures. This time 'terrain' was the subject, and I found his insight unusually profound for a race we are all too ready to write off as 'barbarians'.

– V.

CUTS ACROSS THE LAND

Orcs don't go to war alone. We like plenty of company. Sometimes we take a dozen mates, and sometimes we take a dozen tribes. Our allies are many, from the mighty *akuun* to the lowliest goblin, sometimes even scarcely reliable human mercenaries. However, there's one ally that's even more untrustworthy than a human, and that is the land itself.

FORESTS

In the old times, before human tribes arrived from beyond the mountains, orcs and elves lived as nomads. Both races lived off the land and both races foraged for fruit and vegetables.[1] The forests are the sole domain of the elves in these times, and it's an arse-headed orc that ventures into the trees in full daylight. Forests are to be avoided, especially by young orcs who ain't big enough to hold a sword. Remember: elves will kill anything with green skin – females, young 'uns, goblins. It's all the same to them.

The reason forests are so dangerous is because of the scouts that patrol them. Even tracts of forest that seem impassable are checked on. Some orcs will tell you that elf scouts appear any time that three trees grow side by side. This is bit fanciful for my tastes; even the best scout can't be everywhere at once, even if it often seems like it. Elf scouts cause all manner of arse-ache, but mainly they report back to their leaders.[2] The enemy will know that your forces are approaching without you ever seeing

1 It would be easy to assume that orcs were a purely carnivorous race, but they do supplement their diet with a meagre selection of vegetables. Fruit is very popular, even causing the odd brawl to break out over small stashes of grapes or apples. It is my guess that while the orcs love meat, they also have a sweet tooth.

2 'To cause an arse-ache' is an expression on a par with 'to cause a headache', which means to vex or to create a problem. Orcs' speech is obsessed with the 'arse', which seems to be a consistent source of discomfort to them, probably on account of all the meat they consume. They are less preoccupied with their brains. No great surprise there.

them. And more than that, they'll know how many orcs you have, what they're armed with, and whether you've got a shaman with you. I sometimes think elf scouts know the make-up of our tribes better than we do.

It's for this reason I like to force-march my warriors through the night and attack forests at first dawn. Elves hate surprises and there's not much I enjoy more than seeing an elf twisting with indecision. Except of course when he's twisting from a rope, hanging from a tall tree. By the neck. For some reason a lot of the elves sit around staring into space in the morning. They're not asleep exactly, but they're definitely up to something. This is the best time to take them unawares.

Should you find yourself attacking elves on their pre-ferred territory, you'll want to bring plenty of torches with you. It's only by setting fire to the trees that you'll distract the enemy long enough to stand a chance against their archers.

Tribes that need wood to build new wagons or fashion spear shafts should obtain it under darkness, avoiding a direct confrontation wherever possible. This isn't really in the orc character, so I often hire small teams of goblins to enter the forests and steal wood. Goblins are noc-turnal, so they'll be grateful for the opportunity to avoid sunlight. However, goblins aren't so good at felling trees, so it's well worth sending a couple of orcs along with big axes. Which is another reason I like axes so much. Did I tell you how much I like an axe?[3]

3 More times than is easily relatable through the simple medium of footnotes, I can assure you, dear reader.

The Great South-eastern Forest

What most *Khagan* won't tell you, and what orcs don't like to talk about, is the Great South-eastern Forest.[4] Something worse than elves live within the deep darkness of that forbidden place. These trees provide shelter to the orcs' most hated foes.

Our ab-dead selves.

Some time before the Asaanic War was truly under way, dark spirits were attacking the living, or worrying at the corpses of the nearly dead. The most brazen of them came at night – only large campfires and plenty of noise kept them at bay, and even then, not always. Others could be found searching the battlefield after a conflict. At first we thought them hungry ghosts – orcs who'd not had enough to eat in life and had returned for one last feast. How wrong we were. The orcs killed by the dark spirits began a new life. An un-life.[5] Rather than give their bodies back to the mud, the *Khasts* rise again to feast on the living. It is our greatest shame that sturdy orc flesh could be so easily corrupted by an angry shade. This is why we avoid the Great South-eastern Forest, so the blight doesn't spread to all orcs.[6]

4 Known to humans as Umber Reach, that fetid and vine-choked place of unnerving evil east of Anghoul and Aurilem.

5 The orcs refer to these risen dead as *Khasts*, although the 'K' is often very guttural, coming off as 'g' sound instead. The dwarves by contrast call these abominations 'ghouls', while the *aelfir* have named them 'drunes'.

6 This explains why Hoim and the market towns surrounding the city are largely free from orc interference. It also lends credence to why the citizens of Anghoul and Aurilem are so suspicious and enforce rigorous curfews after sunset.

WETLANDS

Swamp ain't good for nothing. There's no one lives there, so you can't raid in a swamp. Auroch don't roam there, wolves don't hunt there and even the fish are scarce. The only reason to venture into the wetlands at all is to head back to the Diresand Desert, and there's little point in doing that unless you're keen to starve to death. What makes the wetlands worse is the hauntings. Even in daylight there is a fell mist and all manner of malevolent spirits lurk. Even the stones themselves are haunted in the wetlands, crying out like witchling elves.[7] Far better to avoid the wetlands altogether. Whole tribes have disappeared in those clinging mists, never to be seen again.

PLAINS

The plains are where the orc feels most at home. We thrive in the gentle breeze, spread like wildfire, not constrained by hill, or summit or boughs. It's also our preferred field of battle, assuming, of course, the tribe, or tribes, outnumber the enemy. Difficult terrain, for the most part, confuses orcs. Letting your warriors fight on uninterrupted grassland is a blessing. It's hard enough to stop them arguing with each other long enough to give the enemy a proper beating, without adding in elements

7 Kani is of course referring to the Shraine Korá, or Keening Stones, of the elves, set in place to confuse the many water spirits who seek to lure unwary travellers to an early death. You can read more about these in Chapter 6 of *The Aelfir Art of War*.

of terrain. It only gives them something else to argue about, and something else for the *Khagi* to get wrong.

The only time a tor, hill or copse are of much use is in the evening, when they provide some element of protection or concealment. Camping out in the open invites attack from any direction. Far better to give your opponent fewer options and your guards and scouts fewer angles to keep watch over. A *Khagan* who wants a quiet life keeps his tribe on the plains whenever he can.

Many *Khagan* direct their tribes where the plains meet the foothills. This is the old wisdom, and a useful thing it is too. By travelling in this way you cut down the directions you can be charged from by cavalry. Elves are often seen crossing the plains, and always escorted by their highest and mightiest.[8] Only a fool tries to charge an enemy from the foothills, so they are effectively a shield for the whole tribe. If the enemy catches you unawares you have the option of falling back to the hills. Send the females and young 'uns off first. Once they're safe get your warriors to fall back too, but only after they've had a chance to give someone a kicking. If they don't get the chance for a scrap they'll be surly for weeks.[9]

8 That is to say cavalry. Elven funeral processions to Korlasia are always escorted by horsemen and the most senior units available. Despite this, the orcs just can't resist attacking, often suffering grievous casualties. The orcs know that defiling elven dead causes great upset to their most hated enemy.

9 It's an incontrovertible truth that the only thing worse to an orc than not fighting is to miss out on the chance to have a fight. This is cause for a great deal of orc misery, which given time transmutes into anger, anger which is often vented on other tribe members. Or human mercenaries.

MOUNTAINS

Mountains are to dwarves what forests are to elves. You have to be equally careful when taking the tribe above the foothills. If you do need to go into the mountains you should get yourself a handful of goblins who are familiar with the area. Don't let anyone eat the little fellers; far better to listen to their advice on the best paths and passes. Fortunately, dwarves tend to stay put in their fortresses. Sending out scouts isn't really in the dwarf spirit; they'd much rather sit in the dark counting their gold by candlelight or trying to invent jokes.[10] There's not much call for orcs to venture into the mountains. There's not much to eat up there and dwarf gold is of little use to anyone. Worse yet is the interminable cold. Better to stay on the plains.

Another reason to stay out of the mountains is the *whyrda*.[11] Plenty of orcs like to argue that *akuun* are *whyrda*, but I'm not convinced. *Whyrda* take many

---

10 The orcs, whom I found to be an entirely humourless race of creatures, are totally convinced that the dwarves have no sense of humour at all. The orcs often tell each other 'dwarf jokes', which are patently unfunny. Apparently, these 'jokes' are what dwarves pass off as humour. Orc jokes by comparison usually involve a kick to the privates, a gentle stabbing, or an insightful commentary on someone's mother.

11 I believe the *Khagan* was referring to the various water spirits and sprites that the dwarves refer to as Vaettir. These comprise of Ruszalkai, Vodyniir, Nockiir and Huldurfolka. It is little wonder the dwarves make citadels with so many dangerous creatures abroad in the mountains. These spirits are also covered in *The Dwarven Field Manual*.

forms, from small *daginn*, to troikas of cloaked women.[12] Avoid them all when you can, and get your shaman to sort it out when you can't. A shaman who can't sort out one or two *whyrda* needs a good kicking. Many a trickster has come unstuck when asked to prove his worth when the tribe are being harassed by a w*hyrda*.

If you're not in the mountains to lure an *akuun* into a binding, then chances are you're there to besiege a dwarf stronghold. This is going to cost you. Supplies, lives, reputation and probably a bit of respect. Often a broken kneecap too, because, you know, fighting dwarves is like that. Many orcs like to say, 'Dying is easy; it's sieges what's hard.' Never, ever, go in through the front gates. The dwarf has had hundreds of years to prepare all sorts of ways to crush, burn, bludgeon and slice attacking forces into tiny pieces. And you can't burn their doors down because the doors are made of stone.

The only way to lay siege to a dwarf fortress is by attacking it at several points at the same time. There'll always be a side door, frequently two. These will be in addition to forgotten waterways and abandoned caves in the lower levels. Make sure you find out every way you can gain entry before giving the order to attack. Goblins are your friends here, and laying siege without them has cost many a *Khagan* the respect of his tribe, often his leadership, and sometimes his life.

---

12 The *Khagan* was of course making reference to the Ruiirmaiden, who have a long and complicated relationship with the dwarves. Some say the fortress of Century Falls would not exist had it not been for the Ruiirmaiden's interference. You can read more about them in my translation of *The Dwarven Field Manual.*

DESERT

A lot of orcs take the old myths very seriously, and it would be nice to believe we're really born from the forest and brush fires of the south. However, there is one distinct truth that no one can deny: orcs need to drink water just like everyone else.

A lot of *Khagan* have forgotten how dangerous a desert is. Water is a precious thing, so make it your priority. Fortunately there's very little call for fighting in deserts. If an orc tribe does get into combat it will most likely face other orcs, who are desperate for supplies. This is when the more carnivorous nature of the orc comes to the fore. There are, however, more conventional ways to cheat death. Drawing off small amounts of auroch blood is one way of keeping your thirst at bay. Auroch blood has a very strong taste, and you'll want to wash it down with water. This is a problem, because if you had any water to wash it down with you wouldn't be drinking blood in the first place.

Second is goats' milk. These surly buggers have all sorts of uses, but it's their milk that really keeps an orc tribe going.[13] Make sure the young 'uns get goats' milk every day, else they grow up with little pansy elf bones. These milk-starved orcs will be neither shite nor dung in five or ten years' time, when you need them to give

13 I am so heartily sick of goats. From the way they eat everything in sight (including my tent), to the way orcs insist on cooking with them. Fermented goat's milk is something no human should have to endure, and the horror of drinking of it is only surpassed by the hangover one suffers the next day. I have already written to the King asking him to make this concoction illegal.

someone a kicking. Whole tribes have dispersed because of one season where the young 'uns didn't get cared for properly, and it almost always happens in the desert.

7

GOBLINS AND OTHER SCUM

*O*nce we had made winter camp, Kani took the time to explain the orcs' relationship with the mountain-dwelling goblins, who sometimes fight alongside the larger orcs.

– V.

NEITHER SHITE NOR DUNG

Many *Khagan* will tell you that a goblin is just a crap kind of orc. Some orcs say that goblins is what happens when you leave an orc in a room with a dwarf woman. Elves say that goblins are the mistakes of orcs and men. Wherever it is the goblins come from, no one really cares, and many *Khagan* won't have them anywhere near their tribe unless supplies are running short. A lot of orcs will tell you that goblins are just a pain in the arse. I disagree on this point, and now I'm going to tell you why.

STRENGTH OF NUMBERS

The only thing that breeds faster than rabbits is orcs, and the only thing that breeds faster than orcs is goblins. Rabbits, goblins – I've eaten both in my time – but goblins do have their uses. Putting goblins down the front won't cause the enemy to flee in mindless panic. No one ever fled from a goblin advance. What it will do is soften up the enemy units. And, as the enemy engage with the goblins, a thought will occur to them – 'This is just the first wave, the orcs are coming next.'[1] This is demoralising for anyone except a dwarf, who loves the opportunity to give someone a kicking almost as much as orcs do. A massed army of orcs, preceded by countless goblins, is a terrible thing to witness, especially if you're a pathetic human.

SHORT BUT POINTY

Another thing I like about goblins is that they slow the enemy down. It's next to impossible to charge through six ranks of goblins without one of them sticking a spear in your horse.[2] This alone makes them useful by my

1 Although Kani Breakspeare would never come out and say it, I got the distinct feeling he had a grudging respect for the dwarves. Culturally they couldn't be more different, but the dwarves' bloody-mindedness appealed to the *Ur-Khagan*, especially their reluctance to retreat.

2 Comments like these make one assume that orcs have a callous disregard for the lives of goblins, which is entirely accurate. While I am no friend to goblins, the orc attitude to their smaller kin never failed to shock me. Often goblins are viewed as little more than a mobile sort of dinner. Only the Grey Riders were afforded some prestige among the tribes who employed them.

reckoning. Anything that stops heavy horse charging your orcs is a boon, and shouldn't be disregarded. The momentum of a cavalry charge will be reduced on the rare occasions a unit of horse does make it through the goblins. This is when your orcs can step in and cut the horses out from under the riders. Often the attacking cavalry will need a few seconds to form up after breaking through. This is when you counter-charge with orcs.

SNEAKY AND TRICKSY

It's often forgotten that goblins can see in the dark much better than orcs and humans. Goblins prefer the night time. A good *Khagan* sends goblins ahead of the main army during the night and orders them to report back at dawn. Goblin scouts are quick, quiet and reliable, if you make the right promises. Promises like not having to fight the following day. Goblins hate daylight, so use this to your advantage when bargaining with them.

Goblin scouts can attack enemy supply trains, though with mixed outcomes. They're better at setting fires behind enemy lines and causing trouble.[3] A lot of orcs complain that fighting like this isn't in the spirit of the Harrowing, but a bit of confusion in the enemy camp is all to the good of the orcs down the front by my reckoning.

3 The human term 'gremlin' is generally used by the citizens of the Arendsonn Kingdom. Goblins are renowned for sabotaging windmills, loosening wagon wheels and any act of arson. Many blocked chimneys have also been blamed on gremlins and even the occasional unwanted pregnancy, which is a thought too horrible to entertain.

GOBLIN DISCIPLINE

Most goblins fighting alongside the tribe care about two things: a share of the spoils and not getting dead. Goblins aren't as interested in prestige as orcs and they rarely have ambitions. Often you'll want to assign a *Khagi* to make sure the goblins don't get out of hand. The *Khagi* will hate you for it, but you can avoid arguments between the goblins and your orcs like this. Don't let goblins near an *akuun*, even a bound one; the *akuun* won't be able to resist, helping himself to a mouthful of goblin quick as you like. This is bad for morale; the goblins will get proper spooked when they see their mates being swallowed whole. Goblins should be dinner *or* mercenaries, but never both at the same time.

GOBLIN SHAMANS

Where the orcs have a *Khagan* to lead a tribe the goblins are led by a shaman. A goblin shaman doesn't really lead, but does have plenty of influence. Asking a goblin shaman to join your tribe for an upcoming battle is a problematic affair. First, you have to promise not to eat them or anyone they know, which is fair enough. Second, you have to offer them tribute. Many *Khagan* can't be doing with this, thinking they're too good for it, but an orc's idea of tribute and a goblin's idea of tribute are two different things. Quite often you can get a proper chat with a goblin shaman for a collection of dead ravens, live snakes or a handful of spiders what aren't too crushed. Goblins love spiders. Don't bother giving them weapons or anything valuable – it's just a waste. Once tribute has been paid you are free to try to employ the goblin shaman and his tribe for future battles. Goblins aren't much different to orcs, so you'll need to divide up the spoils just like you would with an orc tribe. Goblin shamans are a little bit cleverer than most goblins and they have real magic on their side too.

MOUNTAIN MAGIC

A goblin shaman can summon swarms of bats from the deep caves of their mountain homes. Not just a dozen bats, or a dozen dozen, but absolutely hundreds of the flappy things.[4] This doesn't sound impressive by itself, but the bats cause unease in the enemy ranks. Bats also create a cloud cover of a sort for the goblins to fight under.[5] Goblins hate daylight, so any additional darkness is a boon for them. Bats also inflict bites on the opposing army, which quickly fester and become infected.

The other area that goblin shaman excel in is rats. Some of them are as big as cats. Goblins use them for food, but they're also good for scurrying into besieged towns. Once inside, the rats can gnaw on supplies, spread

4 Goblin and orc counting seems largely based on the idea that when you run out of fingers and ears to count on you should start over, hence the obsession with dozens. When I tried to explain to them that counting in tens was easier they looked disgusted and told me that anything less than a dozen 'was not to be trusted'.

5 This gives rise to the Arend expression: 'It's a fell wind that blows dark on a summer's day.' The fell wind is in fact the bats as they swarm ahead of the orcs and goblins, who frequently attack at the height of summer.

disease, and generally wear down the morale of the defenders. Elves in particular hate rats, especially the elf women who stand on chairs and get weepy.

While not magic in the strictest sense, goblin shaman also rear giant spiders. They breed these eight-legged brutes purely for size, and feed them birds and mice. Many *Khagan* will stipulate a goblin tribe leaves the bloody spiders at home as they spook the orcs something rotten. There's also the problem that spiders are usually poisonous, which causes havoc in the camp.[6] Goblin shamans are obsessed with growing larger and larger spiders, but won't tell anyone why. Most orcs put it down to living in the mountains too long.[7]

In addition to these strange talents, goblin shamans also have mastery over mountain wolves. Some tales are told of shamans that can speak with the wolves. Other stories tell of giant wolves that can speak in orc and goblin. Seems a bit of a stretch to be honest, but weirder things happen. It's this friendship with the wolves that brings me to the greatest use for goblins.

6 When Kani Breakspeare speaks of havoc, what he actually means is disruption. Poison doesn't affect orcs like it does humans. A bite from a spider can cause death for a human in a matter of minutes. Orcs by contrast merely lose control of their bowels for a day or two.

7 A popular goblin pastime is to pit these giant spiders against each other for sport. Huge bets rest on the outcomes of these horrific fights. Some of the creatures are larger than rats and they are uniformly venomous.

Although it pains me to say it, goblins are more coopera-
tive than your average orc. Maybe it's because they're
weaker, maybe it's because they're smaller, who knows?
The fact remains that goblins work together to survive.[8]
The cooperation isn't just limited to goblins of the same
tribe, but of differing tribes, who communicate with each
other. Goblins have used messengers for a long time, but
they gained a marked increase in respect when they
mastered wolves and rode across the mountains.

An orc ain't got no use for a horse except for eating it.
Trying to get horses to take an order from an orc is like
asking a human not to shit his pants.[9] The one major
failing of an orc army is that we have no heavy horse. But
what we do have are goblins on wolves, or the Grey
Riders, as they're known.

Grey Riders are not well trained, nor are they particularly brave or possessed of stunning strategy. They do
cause a lot of confusion and can harass an enemy's
flanks, making the opposing leader wary of committing
his troops in the centre. Grey Riders tend to fight in a
loose skirmish formation, not because they're clever, just

8 This isn't strictly true. Goblins are loathsome and selfish creatures who
prey on each other in the blink of an eye. However, when compared to orcs
they are paragons of organisation and cooperation. Goblins don't give in to
internecine bickering in the midst of battle, but rather they foster a pack
mentality not unlike the rats they are so fond of.

9 This is not an orc critique of human incontinence, rather the propensity
for human soldiers to lose control of their bowels when in battle. Orc bowels
by contrast appear to be made of cast iron, like their guts. And their brains.

because they can't ride side by side like proper, trained horse riders. This works to their advantage as enemy cavalry can't counter-charge them easily.

One or two Grey Riders by themselves are no big threat. They're like wasps buzzing about at dinner time. No great arse-ache. Several dozen Grey Riders are a different matter. The wolf-mounted goblins can have plenty of short bows behind the enemy line in a matter of minutes. The carefully laid plans of the enemy general go up in flames when a pack of snarling wolves start attacking the less armoured units, such as elf archers. Or elf choirs.

The goblins have tried to breed larger wolves for some time now, but putting an orc on a wolf usually ends in disaster. Disaster that sees the orc recovering from bite wounds for the following week.[10] The larger the wolves get, the more surly they are, and less likely to take a rider. Wolves look set to be only manageable by the goblins, and that's why it's worth taking the time to include the smaller kin in our plans.

HUMAN MERCENARIES

I've never really understood humans. They seem to invent new rules for themselves as they go along, forgetting what came before as soon as they grow bored. They're not particularly good in a fight. They make a few

10 The Grey Riders' wolves are like a thing from nightmare. Standing over three feet tall and almost seven feet long, they have a wily patience that is unnerving in a supposedly wild creature. Tales of red-eyed, rabid monstrosities stalking lonely farmsteads are entirely plausible to me after seeing these great beasts first-hand.

passable objects. Mainly they're good for growing food and better at being food.

Somewhere down the ages a clever and vicious little bastard realised that orcs never take money from the places we raze. We raid a place for food, for wood, for the fun of the fight, and because we like to set fire to things. Gold, silver and all that other nonsense has no place in orc culture. Only steel has any real meaning, and that's something all races have in common. This clever human bastard had his own reasons for turning on his own and selling his sword to fight alongside the orcs, but chief among them was earning lots of money.[11]

Human mercenaries will work for an orc *Khagan* on the agreement they get the money that's left lying around

11 No one knows who the first human mercenaries were, and because the orcs don't keep written records we never will. I would postulate that it's the Arends started the whole sorry business, due to the human mercenary's penchant for woad and war paint decoration. Certainly all of the humans employed for Kani were from the Arendsonn Kingdom.

after a raid. And no one eats them. This contract only lasts as long as the human is alive.[12] Often the humans will try to make themselves look as fierce as the orcs, which makes some orcs laugh. It annoys the piss out of me.[13] They blacken their faces and make their hair stick up. They plait animal skulls into their beards and tattoo themselves blue. Sometimes it's difficult remembering they're the same humans who live on farms and have those little wriggly pink young 'uns.

Humans can ride horses, and even a small group of fighters on horseback can make all the difference during a large battle. You can also use them as scouts, riding ahead of the tribe and looking out for trouble. This suits everyone best. The orcs don't get fidgety and hungry, and the humans don't have to feel nervous about getting ate all day long. You'll want to keep the camps spaced apart at night too. The thought of all that meat just snoring away under the stars is too much for some orcs, especially when things are bad and there ain't much food about. I've taken to keeping a small stash of money with me just in case I need to hire some mercenaries. Not that I need to with three tribes of orcs round me, but you never know.

12 Note that orcs don't actually write contracts. None of them can read, much less write. A *Khagan*'s word is unbreakable, and if he says that no one can eat the human mercenaries then that is what happens. Orcs who go against the *Khagan*'s contract usually end up spitted on poles. *Khagan* who break their word suffer the same fate. In an otherwise chaotic and dangerous environment, the *Khagan*'s word offers a degree of absolute stability.

13 The many aspects of humans that annoyed Kani Breakspeare could easily fill the pages of a small book. I still struggle to accept he even spoke to me during my long months among the orcs, let alone recounted his approach to war and the attitudes of the orcs.

8

TROLLS AND SHAMAN

Although Kani made it clear that he didn't trust sha-mans, he did have one serving him. What follows is his response to my asking him why it was necessary to have these eccentric individuals present.

– V.

A NEW POWER

We orcs have become more organised since the shamans acquired their new powers. The shamans encourage the *Khagan* to attract more orcs to their tribes. Orcs are numerous, but a faster way to build a tribe's strength is to recruit Odds, or randoms as some orcs like to call them. Odds can be goblins, *akuun*, the shamans them-selves, even human mercenaries. They all have their uses, even humans, though it annoys me to say it. By far the most destructive of all the Odds are the *akuun*.

The Akuun

Akuun have always been feral and untameable.[1] A troll is just as likely to kill and eat an orc as he is a human. The only thing trolls like to eat more than humans and orcs is goblins. In the old times a *Khagan* would try to bribe *akuun* into fighting for him. Usually this took the form of tying half a dozen goblins to a post in the foothills of the mountains. The *Khagan* would then make a lot of noise to alert the nearby *akuun*. Quite a few tribes discovered they needed a new *Khagan* after this. The *akuun* would eat not just the bribe but the *Khagan* offering it too.

This ravenous appetite has stopped the *akuun* forming any sort of proper alliance with the orcs for hundreds and hundreds of years.[2] The trolls have been a grave threat to those venturing into the mountains for as long as anyone can remember. Some say they are as old as the *daginn*. Dwarves have a long history of turning back trolls from the gates of their underground cities, but

1 *Akuun* is the orc name for troll. Many of my esteemed colleagues in Hoim may believe mountain trolls are but folk tales. I can, however, assure them this is not the case. Trolls are not simply 'really big orcs', but living siege engines that roam the mountains and foothills attempting to sate their extraordinary appetites. I can also lay to rest any claim that trolls turn to stone in sunlight. This is fanciful nonsense. Trolls are naturally nocturnal, but obey their shaman any time of the day or night.

2 Although I never found any hard evidence of it I am fairly sure orc counting becomes increasingly vague after about nine hundred. It's not that orcs are too stupid to conceive a number greater than a thousand, they just lose interest – hence 'hundreds and hundreds'. Also a 'dozen-hundred' is a popular figure in orc language.

they aren't always successful. The only thing worse than a horde of goblins is a troika of trolls, and the dwarves live in fear of times when the trolls gather in this fashion.[3] This is why it's useful to take a handful of the huge brutes if you plan to lay siege to the short bastards. The *aelfir* protection of their burial grounds and forests brings them into contact with the *akuun*. Less common are trolls who plunder the northern trade route, and prey on human and dwarf caravans.

Trolls can be found all over Naer Evain, from the Friegunn Wetlands to the Scarsfaalen Forest, but they always return to the mountains in winter. We reckon they mate with each other during the winter, which is probably about as horrible a thing as any orc can imagine. Many *Khagan* lead their shaman to the *akuun* breeding grounds with the express reason of binding young trolls.

CROLL BINÒING

Since the Time of Teeth, the orc shaman have found a way to master the *akuun*. This is a large part of the shamans' rise to power in recent years. The shamans say they bind the spirit of fire to a particular troll, which curbs its more carnivorous impulses. Most orcs assume

3 Trolls, while largely solitary, have been known to band together for shared gain. This particular low-level cunning and cooperation results in a troika of trolls. No one knows why they always gather in threes. I asked if a troika might be a family unit, but the orcs simply laughed at me and asked if I'd been on the mushrooms. The idea that trolls would live together as a family was utterly unthinkable to the orcs, who have a hard time tolerating each other.

that when a troll is bound, a *Khagan* can instruct it to do something useful, like smash down gates to a walled town. This isn't entirely true. In fact, the *Khagan* must ask the shaman to order the *akuun*. The shaman demands quite a hefty share of the spoils for this unique talent and his prestige is swelled considerably.

TROLLS IN BATTLE

A bound troll is a huge boon to an invading orc army, and it's a salt wind that blows on a *Khagan* who doesn't have a couple under his command during war time. The orcs aspire to be as violent and ferocious as the troll, and are often so awed by its presence they stop fighting each other. Enemy units try to avoid facing the implacable advance of the troll. Infantry will often retreat in disorder rather than fight these awful creatures.[4] You should keep a unit of orcs with spears at hand at all times to defend the *akuun*. The enemy will try to use heavy horse to kill the troll if they have them. Even something fourteen feet tall will keel over if a horse and lance collide with it.

There is no finesse or strategy to using a troll in battle, but you do have to keep an eye on the shaman. A good shaman can keep control of an *akuun* from up to seventy feet, so he'll need to be fairly close to the front. If the shaman should die then you have a real problem on your

4 And rightly so. The best way to dispatch an *akuun*, in my opinion, is with a siege engine from a very great distance. Failing this, you should aim to set fire to them and give them plenty of time to burn. You can read more about dispatching these horrific creatures in my translation of *The Dwarven Field Manual* by Sundin Hallestøm.

hands as the magic that bound the troll unravels. A young troll will most likely sit down and stare at the grass. They're easily confused at that age, and being unbound is as confusing as it gets. An older troll will immediately go on the rampage. What it can't eat it will kill, and what it can't kill it will maim. Enemies or nearby orcs, wolves, horses, buildings, even large rocks, it's all the same to a troll on the rampage.[5] A dead shaman is a real pain in the arse, but there are precautions you can take.

ORC SHAMANS

For a long time shamans were simply story tellers and recorders of myth.[6] They were tolerated at best, and most orcs assumed there was something not right with them. Many orc shamans would cast bits of old bone in the dust and claim to tell futures. Some would gut birds and stare at the entrails. Orcs, who are not overly concerned

5 Troll rampages accounted for a large number of casualties at the end of the Battle of Salt Wind. It was the death of the shamans who controlled the trolls that made any attempt at rallying the tribes untenable. This reliance on shamans is the cause of much friction. *Khagan* dislike being dependent on anyone.

6 Orc shamans are a diverse lot, and can be male or female. They keep the population in their thrall with a heady mixture of theatrics, superstition and, dare I say, actual magic on occasion. I did, however, witness the 'troll binding' ceremony that Kani mentioned. I do not believe that the shamans bind the trolls with a fire spirit from the orc creation myths as they say they do. It is my guess the shaman have found a way of bargaining with the Umbral Wraiths for control over these mighty mountain creatures. Whether this misdirection by the shaman is intended or not, it does beg the question of whether the Umbral Wraiths have some larger plan afoot.

by the future, outside of what's for dinner, became rapt with these petty ceremonies. Many shamans became rich in this fashion, which brought them into conflict with the *Khagan*. Others would light large fires and urge the orcs in the tribe to become one with the flames. Orcs are born of the inferno, but only in the myths. They're not immune to fire, no matter how persuasive the shaman is. Having to wake up to burnt and hungover orcs is a problem no *Khagan* really needs, especially if it's the day before a big battle.

Shamans were largely a bloody nuisance and they often declined to fight like regular orcs, so that they could 'compose tales of the battle'. Pretty hard to retell stories of the great battles if you're dead, they argued. This was probably the soundest line of thought many of them had. Many tribes refused to have shamans in their midst, especially those orcs near the Bitterfang Mountains and the Kourgaad Pass. If an orc started getting funny ideas he'd get an arse-kicking and be left on the plains by himself.[7]

AFTER THE TIME OF TEETH

Something happened during the Time of Teeth and the shamans started casting real spells. Up until that point

---

7 Arse-kicking is a much greater part of orc culture than the name implies. An orc is ejected if it fails to meet the expectations of his tribe. Every orc in the tribe then makes it his business to deliver a single kick to the offending orc's hindquarters. Quite often this sustained assault results in the ejected orc suffering a broken pelvis or fractured thighs. At the very least he won't be able to sit down for a month. I suspect it is for this reason that orc shamans are very fast when running.

shaman magic was largely putting acorns in the firewood to make popping noises and throwing handfuls of minerals around to make purple and green 'magic'. The days of lies and nonsense were over; the shamans had finally discovered a power of their own. And it didn't go down too well with the *Khagan*, who have enough to think about.

A few shamans can genuinely see the future, although they need a lot of mushrooms to get properly into one of their 'trances'. Other shamans can inspire fear in our enemies with just a look, something we call the Bale-gaze or the Dark-eye. These shamans usually have a large retinue and dress in outlandish costumes. However, the greatest power of an orc shaman is their ability to bargain with the spirits of fire. All shamans master this ability, usually after long periods of apprenticeship. They bind a fire spirit to an *akuun* and from then on the *akuun* will obey commands, just like a regular orc. No *Khagan* can ignore such power, and anyone attempting a large battle needs to have a few shamans on his side.

There is another power that the shamans don't talk about, and yet it is one every *Khagan* needs to be wary of. Orcs are easily impressed by things they don't understand. Some say the foundation of orc culture is taking orders from other orcs who 'get it' more than you do. Shamans get very excited about titles and adopt flamboyant names for themselves. This in turn attracts followers. In large numbers these followers become retinues, and if a *Khagan* belongs to a tribe with an influential shaman, he might come unstuck. The first and last word in any tribe should come from the *Khagan*. You shouldn't have to repeat yourself twice, and you should never discuss what needs doing in front of the tribe. This breeds doubt. Your retinue must always be bigger than the shaman's, or you'll look weak in front of your tribe.

USING ShAMANS IN BATTLE

If you've got an *akuun* fighting with your orcs, you need to keep the shaman alive. This is less hard than it sounds, as he'll have a big retinue of weirdos and worshippers. A shaman's retinue can be almost as deadly as a unit of berserkers. They'll die laughing to keep the shaman alive, and won't think twice about sacrificing themselves. Like I say, weirdos.

A shaman can cause entire enemy units to run away with a single look. Only elves seem to have a measure of willpower against this magic. A shaman also inspires the orcs nearby to fight twice as hard. A shaman working together with his *Khagan* is an unbeatable combination, just as orcs working with *akuun* is a force without reckoning. However, most shamans covet the title and authority of a *Khagan*, so it's difficult to trust the spooky buggers.

BERSERKERS

Many humans will tell you that every warrior in an orc army is a berserker. Everyone except the goblins, who shit their pants at the first sign of trouble. This ain't the whole truth of it. Orcs, while bloody ferocious, don't lose complete control of their senses, nor do they stop feeling pain. A good orc can still take orders and will pull

back if his *Khagi* can shout loud enough over the din of battle. Berserkers are an entirely different matter.

It's no secret that the orc bloodline is anything but pure. Half-breeds exist and even thrive in some corners of Naer Evain.[8] The most profound change occurs when orc blood has some *akuun* blood in it. Asaan Firebringer had it, I have it, and so do plenty of other orcs, a lot of whom have risen to the position of *Khagan*. There are some orcs who have slightly more *akuun* blood in them than is proper; they might be actual half-breeds or they

8 Half-breed is a very ambiguous term when applied to the mathematically challenged orcs. For example: Kani Breakspeare considers himself a half-breed, but when I examined his family tree I discovered he was only one-eighth *akuun*. Berserkers tend to be one-quarter *akuun*. Actual orc-*akuun* half-breeds are intensely stupid and very dangerous.

might just have been born angry. These types of orcs are given to the tribe shaman at a young age and become part of his retinue. No one really knows what the shamans do to the young orcs, but before long they are massive, often reaching eight feet tall. What they make up for in height and ferocity they lack in discipline or any forethought, not that orcs ever had a great deal of that.

Berserkers often take to the field naked as the day they were born, wielding two-handed weapons and shouting incoherent abuse that turns the air blue. Their skin has been hardened under a hundred-dozen punishments by the shaman, and they sweat and writhe with barely contained fury. Berserkers are much like the *akuun* whom they were sired from, and share an appetite for goblins, and even orcs. These maniacs can take wounds that would kill other orcs outright, and are the true face of the consuming fire of old legend.

Berserkers obey no orders. An army must simply work around them. The enemy will be shocked and sickened by the violence that just one orc can mete out. Very rarely a berserker will become so enraged he will turn upon his own kin. This is unfortunate, and even the shamans can't control these acts of madness. It's for this reason that many *Khagan* prefer to send berserkers ahead of the main advance. Other *Khagan* have sent small numbers of berserkers into enemy encampments under the cover of darkness. This seems like a waste of their talents, but does prevent the possibility of the berserkers turning on the regular orcs fighting alongside them. A *Khagan* shouldn't expect these lunatics to last more than a single battle. These orcs were given to the shamans because they are unwanted. They know this, and they seek their own deaths on the blades of our enemies. A berserker's only pleasure is making sure as many enemies fall beneath his blade as is possible. A berserker should be down the front from the first opportunity and given a wide berth should he survive the battle.

Some *Khagan* have veteran berserkers who just don't seem to die. They keep them in large cages and feed them raw meat when there's no one to fight. Personally, I'm not sure there's a cage in the world I'd trust that much, but orcs is orcs, and we all do things different.

9

HISTORICAL ACCOUNT –
THE BATTLE OF SALT WIND

The account was told to me by Kani Breakspeare in the small hours of one morning. He was particularly maudlin following the capture of a good deal of dwarf ale, which had a strange effect on the Khagan.

– V.

A GROWING VIOLENCE

We were around thirty summers old when the Asaanic War began. We didn't call it the Asaanic War back then. It just started out as a bit of fun. My tribe and Asaan's tribe, raiding together. He'd recently come over the Scarlet Fang Mountains and already had a lot of prestige. Neither of us needed to be *Ur-Khagan* because we respected each other. We reaped many prizes in the first three years. Our tribes prospered and grew, the *Khagi* became competent and wise. Our renown spread, retold at the Great Meets of Sour Tongue, Batter and further afield. In time other *Khagan* joined us, lending their banners to ours. After seven years we were seven tribes strong, regularly raiding the towns of the Arends and the Solari. We even attacked Khaershåine, but this was mostly done to deplete the more ambitious tribes. Many *Khagan* who threatened Asaan's dominance died in this way. Everyone wanted an *Ur-Khagan* by now, but none could agree on whom to back and how to decide it. The only reason we attacked Khaershåine at all was because of Asaan's shaman, Ajjall Dogface. I told him that I thought it was crooked, and sending good honest *Khagan* to their deaths wasn't in the spirit of the Harrowing, but Asaan maintained it was for the best. The tribes that were left leaderless held challenges for new, less charismatic *Khagan*. Some were absorbed by the other tribes. In time only Asaan and myself remained from the original *Khagan*.

Asaan was made *Ur-Khagan* the following year. It might have been me in command but for Dogface, who knew a thing or two about persuading orcs. Dogface made deals with the *Khagan* of the five tribes to lend their support, and it came to pass that Asaan Firebringer became *Ur-Khagan*, without having to fight anyone for the honour. Not even me, I'm ashamed to say. And still more tribes flocked to his banner.

COTAL WAR COMES CO NAER EVAIN

We attacked everywhere, the Arends and the Solari alike. The dwarves in their citadels knew no rest, particularly those at Century Falls. Even the forests of the elves were sacked. We were ascendant, and Asaan promised a red rain when we exterminated all those who opposed us. Seven years stretched into twelve, became twenty-four. Some shamans foretold victory in the thirty-sixth year of the war.[1] Confidence was high; we felt invincible. And yet with each passing day, Asaan fell more deeply under the influence of Ajjall Dogface.

Suddenly our plans changed. We were turning away from the Solari and the Arends, due to travel across the Kourgaad Plains and meet several tribes of goblins and orcs. None of it made much sense to me, but Asaan assured me we were going to get even with the elves once and for all. We were going to make them pay a price in blood for denying us audience with the Great Mother.

ThE plAN GOES AWRy

Ajjall Dogface had made an alliance by means of his witchery. He told us he was in contact with another shaman called Haelspont, who promised to aid the sack of Naer Khaeris by providing orcs, goblins and a number of *akuun*.[2] I thought it strange this orc had an elf name, but Asaan wouldn't hear my suspicions out. I now know

1 Yet more proof of the orc fascination with the number twelve and counting in dozens. If the orcs ever get around to maintaining any sort of calendar it will undoubtedly feature twelve months to a year and record longer periods in cycles of twelve years.

2 Kani maintains this communication was arcane in nature, rather than by simple messenger, something I struggle to believe. Only the elves can achieve such a feat, and even then at great cost.

Haelspont isn't an orc or elf at all, but something other that neither sleeps nor feeds.[3] He exists to this day, plaguing the dwarves at Voss Colg and Voss Jur, working on fell magics in the abyss beyond the mountains.

The orcs and goblins that Haelspont promised never appeared. Ajjall Dogface made various excuses, none of which seemed very plausible. At first he claimed the dwarves of Voss Jur had finally emerged from their citadel, keen to retake the Scarlet Fang Pass. This sounded unlikely. Dwarves rarely leave the safety of their mountains, and those at Voss Jur lacked strong leadership. Then the shaman told us Haelspont had been attacked. A seasoned group of *aelfir* Drae Ade had infiltrated his stygian home, wounding him badly with magic and skill at arms. I was tired of the excuses by this point, and even Asaan was growing restless. The shaman sensed this, assuring us Haelspont himself was leading the tribes to the Salt Flats. We pressed on, keen to start the battle at Naer Khaeris, fully aware that every *aelfir* who could lift a blade would be there to meet us.[4] One night, when Asaan was the worse for drink, he mentioned he didn't fancy our chances. I questioned him the next day, but he denied

3 The name Haelspont is not unknown to me; he plays a large part in the Battle of Scarlet Fang Pass, which I translate in *The Dwarven Field Manual*. I was present at this battle and witnessed the power of the eldritch sorcerer first-hand. The *aelfir* of Sia Na Roin are also keen to put an end to Haelspont. The Sons of Daellnis in particular desire to venture over the mountains to hunt Haelspont down.

4 Not strictly true. The *aelfir* were spread very thin at this time. Defending the whole of the Great Northern Forest is no small undertaking. I felt it best not to contradict Kani Breakspeare, for reasons concerning my longevity.

it, back in the thrall of Ajjall Dogface and his empty promises.

I was already expecting the next excuse, but I didn't imagine it would be so brazen. Ajjall told us that the dwarves had summoned two golems from the earth itself. The golems had laid waste to the *akuun* we had been promised. Two dozen of them, enough to destroy a city. I stormed out of the tent, keen to be free of the whining shaman. He would be the end of us, I was sure of it. The force that attacked Naer Khaeris was missing a fifth of its strength before we had even begun. Asaan was still keen to begin the extermination of the elves, even without the orcs from beyond the Scarlet Fang Mountains. He couldn't back down; we had travelled so far and the orcs were at fever pitch. To turn back would cast doubts on his leadership. What would begin in Naer Khaeris would come to fruition in Sia Na Roin, said Asaan, nothing less than the complete destruction of every elf that drew breath.

MEAT FOR THE FIRE

Each day brought us closer to Naer Khaeris, and each night gave us the reward of a farmhouse to sack. The elves put up a stiff defence of the farmers, buying time for their fleeing kin. This heroism cost them dearly. The orcs didn't care for the farmers, but welcomed the chance to wear down the elven cavalry. Mainly we hid behind walls of spears and struck back with arrows, but combat was met. Slowly but surely we ground each high-born down into the mud, stamping their arrogant faces to pulp. The tribes dined on horsemeat and the mood remained resolute despite our losses. I found myself believing again, daring to hope we might prevail. The orcs around me had never doubted.

the BaTTLe of SALT WIND

The day had finally come and all the auspices were on our side, or so the shamans kept telling us. The air fairly reeked of bird entrails and all indicating bold fortunes, told to eager orcs thinking themselves invincible. The wind swept down from the west, into the teeth of our enemy, remaining at our back. Asaan insisted we send the goblins first, which upset everyone. Fights were started. None of the tribes wanted to miss out; everyone wanted to be in the first wave. Impossible of course, on account of there being so many of us, but that's orcs for you. Ajjall Dogface had convinced Asaan we needed to wear down the enemy morale, and to do it with goblins. I remember leaving the tent, making my way back to my own retinue, when Asaan caught up with me. I asked him who the *Ur-Khagan* was. He replied, 'It's me, of course.' I stalked away, unconvinced.

the thiRd Day

By the second day my tribe were heartily sick of doing nothing, and I agreed with them. The *Khagan* of the Kourgaad Pass Tribe decided that he too would join the battle, with or without Asaan's permission. While I was content to lead my tribe along the south bank of the river, the Kourgaad Pass Tribe opted to cross it. It was their intent to get around behind Naer Khaeris, cutting off any means of escape and deterring any possible

reinforcements. As orc plans go it was a particularly inspired one, but the *Khagan*, called Khanik Bullneck, was not the most talkative. He failed to mention what he'd planned. The only reason I know his tribe were almost annihilated was because I saw it happen with my own eyes. We'd marched through the night, my tribe on the south bank, his on the north, but as dawn approached it was clear Khanik's plan had faltered. Orcs aren't naturally strong swimmers and a good few were swept away by the current. Many simply drowned. The orcs that did manage the crossing soon wished they hadn't. Keen to flee the punishment of the elven scouts, they tried to swim back. None made it. Most were armoured, or insisted on keeping their blades, which dragged them to their deaths beneath the rushing waters.

My own tribe found the footing difficult. Many lost boots, or became stuck fast. The southern bank of the river had become a morass during the long, wet summer. Dawn of the third day of battle found us frustrated, cold, and covered in mud. We found a small rise and settled there, waiting for the rest of the orc line to catch up with us. And that's when the singing started.

FELL WITCHERY ON THE AIR

Very little instils fear in the orc heart like the sound of elven witchery. Facing cavalry brings a certain grim inevitability, but the singers of the elves are strange and unpredictable. My tribe took to making jokes to bolster their spirits, but I knew full well they were rattled.

Four more orc tribes had been committed along with the last of the goblins who lacked mounts. Grey Riders had led the way, but were a spent force, fleeing to the right flank in the south. The orcs roared and raged at the gates of Naer Khaeris, yet few could believe the unearthly fortunes of the elves. Our archers' attacks were turned aside, as if the arrows were caught in unnatural winds, shafts snapping in mid-air. The elves' own arrows struck us unimpeded. Even the shaman-summoned pall of bats fell from the sky. The high-pitched shriek of the winged vermin drowned out all other sound as leathery wings were trampled into the mud.

That's when the elven High King mounted a counter-charge from the gates themselves. He didn't even bother to ride into battle, content to fight on foot, laying about with that great silver sword of his. Arrogant ponce. Seeing him moving serpent-fast, and wielding a weapon befitting a great leader, I wondered if we could prevail. Shimmering light played about his head like a thousand golden tongues of fire, but it was his face that was truly terrible. His eyes held only death for any orc daring to set his will against the elves.

The High King's retinue were implacable, easily the match of our most seasoned *Khagi*. I suspect they were emboldened by the ceaseless arcane chants of their witches. Nothing unsettled them: not being outnumbered; not the brutal recklessness of the berserkers; not even the terror created by the *akuun*. They were like mountain stones, immovable and unbreakable. They died all too slowly, and meted out wounds fatal and shocking.[5]

5 Kani, in my opinion, is correct in his guess that the High King's retinue would have had arcane support. It is likely they would have been bolstered by an effect called Gravitas, making them all but suicidal in the face of such numerical superiority.

The very act of charging the gates was made treacherous by the bodies of the fallen, who lay groaning and wailing. The High King took great pleasure in finishing any fallen orc within reach. More tribes advanced, keen to win glory, but meeting instead a dark cloud of elven arrows. The archers continued to reap a grim tithe. I saw the beginnings of doubt form on the faces of my *Khagi* and knew I'd be hard-pressed to reassure them. Fortunately I didn't need to, for the *akuun* had arrived.

TORTURES AND TROIKAS

Three groups of them shambled forward, massive and horrible as any *akuun* in memory. All bore great rams and possessed an aura of terrible violence that begged to be let off the leash. The orcs that marched beside them did so warily. Blood was in the air. Even the careful instructions of the shamans wouldn't ensure total obedience. Perhaps it was simply that the *akuun* had their hands full with battering rams, but no goblins or orcs were eaten by their larger kin. Not at first, anyway.

The *akuun* were briefly forgotten as a new threat emerged. Far from my tribe, to the south, or the right flank of our force, human archers attacked. The whole Harrowing shuddered to a standstill as everyone took a moment to turn and regard the commotion. This moment of confusion bought the elven archers more time to rain death on us, but instead of turning back the orcs grew furious. The need for slaughter called out to us like an old friend. And calling out loudest of all was Asaan Firebringer himself, leading the third wave.

Urged on by the arrival of the *Ur-Khagan*, the *akuun*

ran forward to destroy the gates. Surely victory was within our grasp? Surely this would be the turning point of the battle? Again the witchery of the elves determined events. Cruel and icy maidens took to the battlements, directing their dark gazes against the *akuun*, who if not riddled with arrows were consumed with star fire. The last of the battering rams reached the gates, only for the *akuun* carrying it to be cut down by the High King himself.

ASAAN'S VICTORY

By now my own tribe had climbed the walls. My axe was slick with the blood of elves and I had a good vantage point for the combat to come. Asaan walked up to the High King almost casually, only the bleak look in his eye betraying his awful intent. The High King by contrast was not so comfortable. He'd thrown himself from the battlements to face the *akuun*, and the handful of counter-charges had cost him dearly. Even the spirit of an immortal king can tire, it would seem.

They circled each other, raining blows almost too fast to see. Asaan, who normally had speed on his side, could not land a blow on the fleet-footed High King. The elf, on the other hand, could not overcome Asaan's great armour, despite the mighty silver blade he wielded. Never in all my years have I seen two warriors so perfectly matched, and yet so different. Asaan, however, possessed an abundant vigour, whereas the High King was almost spent. Every strike was slower than the last, parries more desperate, each riposte carrying less conviction. And then Asaan trapped the High King's blade between his matched khukri, mashing his forehead into the High King's face with a dreadful smacking sound. This was the moment we had not dared to hope for. The cruellest urges of every orc to have ever lived were suddenly manifested. The High King slumped into the mud, staring upward at the great bulk of Asaan, knowing his end had come. The *Ur-Khagan* let out a mighty shout, then slashed down into the chest of the High King, the khukri piercing his lungs.

short-lived

It was then that more humans broke through our ranks at the rear. Mounted on horses, and bolstered by the few remaining elf cavalry, they charged unchecked and unchallenged. It was a moment sour as the taste of spoiled meat. Below me lay the corpse of the High King, while faithful orc warriors at the rear died in their dozens. Shock and discord ran through the tribes; orders were given, but refused or disobeyed. Fights broke out; discipline faltered. Only those within shouting distance of Asaan held their nerve, keen to spill more elf blood.

the elves are avenged

The High King's retinue were appalled by their loss, but settled into an icy silence. They were as the weapons they wielded: steely, unflinching, unemotional. One among them took it upon herself to guard the High King's body. Slight and nimble she was, bearing the bladed spear so favoured by the elves. She was liberally painted in the blood of our kin, her ruined armour testament to the blows that had struck her. In truth she had no need for such armour. There was a dauntless quality about her, as if the disdain of her gaze could turn aside the hardest of blows.[6]

Asaan Firebringer loomed over her, as an *akuun* looms over a goblin, full of dreadful intensity. She stared up at the hulking *Ur-Khagan*, resolute and resolved. And then he fell on her with all the fury at his disposal. Gone was the careful brutality he had marshalled for the High King. It was as if this female elf's very existence was a deep blasphemy to Asaan. In truth, I simply think he wanted to claim the High King's head. Being denied by this lone retainer soured his spirits.

She was more than just an elf – I truly believe this. Nothing alive moves so fast or attacks so methodically. Her every breath was measured, every step thought through, no attack wasted. Where Asaan struck, she parried and counter-attacked, where he stepped aside she followed up, when he tried to close distance she held him off. Time and again the spear struck, at thighs and knees, ankles and groin. The High King, so keen to behead Asaan Firebringer, had been thwarted by the great, spiked pauldrons. The retainer on the other hand cared not for dramatic victory, just the death of a hated enemy. Asaan's khukri sundered the air and sliced at

6 It is interesting to me that Kani Breakspeare insists Asaan Firebringer's opponent was female, while La Darielle Daellen Staern's account recalls an unnamed male elven warrior facing the *Ur-Khagan*. More interesting still is the fact that La Darielle was the only female member of the High King's retinue that day.

nothing. His strikes became more frenzied and desperate until he discovered one hand had been removed. Staring at the stump of his wrist in awful disbelief, Asaan Fire-bringer, *Ur-Khagan*, friend, greatest leader of all the orcs, prosecutor of the longest Harrowing in orc history, sank to his knees.

And was decapitated.

the salt wind and the wicked sisters

Chaos was total. The air was filled with the anguished cries of orcs and unnatural elven song. The dying carpeted the field. A riot of bloodstained limbs twisted about the corpses of mountain wolves; bodies piled up around massive forms of slain *akuun*. Death lurked at every turn. Determined to press on, I ordered my tribe to capture the gatehouses. They did me proud, hacking and hewing at those elves who held their ground.

To the north, a gathering of the hated elf singers stalked with light feet, accompanied by units of spearmen. The few orcs that rose to meet them were turned back by a terrible despair, in part fuelled by Asaan's untimely end. The singers, led by a dark-haired female elf, routed the remaining northern flank with a dirge full of misery and distress.[7]

My orcs were failing to open the doors of the elf town,

7 Undoubtedly Morrigah Asendilar. One of the triplets and the most enigmatic daughter of the High King. Being able to imbue enemies with despair is one of many mystical effects employed by the elves. You can read more about this in Chapter 8 of *The Aelfir Art of War*, also available in the central library of Hoim.

and paying for each wasted moment in blood. By chance, a troika of *akuun*, part of the fourth wave, drew close, urged on by their shamans. My tribe gave a great cheer. The trolls would give us access to the city, and we could escape the ravages of the cavalry and the massed volleys of arrows. But yet again we were undone by elven witchery.

We became aware of shadowy presences as the light began to fade from the sky. At first we thought the Umber Wraiths had come to feast on the dead, but in truth the elves had found some eldritch way to transform their scouts into shades. We were unable to keep them from their purpose. Blades found no purchase, mauls met no resistance. The ghost-like scouts pressed on, deeper into the heart of the battlefield, and then materialised. This was when they struck our shamans, filling the mystics with slender arrows, ignoring whole retinues to strike at those holding the *akuun* in their sway. The orcs nearby retaliated, making the scouts pay dearly for their insult, but the damage was done. Lacking the guiding minds of the shamans, the remaining *akuun* turned feral.

Defeat was now total.

the crush

At the rear we were cut down and fled. The joint human and elf cavalry made a cruel joke of any resistance. At the front we were at the mercy of the very creatures we had brought to the war. Seeing no point in pressing on, I ordered my tribe to fight their way south, where we found the barges of humans. We waited as long as we could, gathering every orc who could stand, cramming them aboard the long boats. I watched the night stain the sky deep blue as we sailed south, towards the marshes, safe from the predations of horsemen.

I had attracted the remnants of three tribes in the rout, and, in the months that came after, I was named *Ur-Khagan*. The only consolation I could take was that Ajjall Dogface must surely have been slain by the ghostly elven scouts. We had been defeated. By the elven witchery? Most certainly; but also by the ambitions of the shamans, and the volatile nature of the *akuun*. And perhaps, most strangely of all, we had not thought the elves and humans would fight side by side.

10

A SUMMARY OF THE ORCS

BY SEBASTIAN VENGHAUS

My colleagues,

Many humans in Hoim despair of their lot in life, claiming it is altogether too nasty, too brutish and rather short. Hardly surprising when the elves live close by. Human existence pales by comparison with the unsurpassable beauty, sophistication and longevity of the *aelfir*. Such grumbling human fools might like instead to consider the Kingdom of Arendsonn, which preys on a population reduced to serfs under a callous nobility. I imagine the serfs of the Arends look to Hoim in the same light as the citizens of Hoim regard the cities of the elves. However, there is one thing that we can all agree on, regardless of being elf or man, free or serf: life is infinitely better than if we had been born an orc.

I have been faced with many indignities in my life, but never have I been asked to endure such hardships in the service of the King. Living in the presence of orcs was as dangerous as it was undignified. Coarse food, inter-mittent shelter, sparse rest and the threat of ever-present violence all take their toll. At first, it seems nothing is sacred to the orcs, from their ideas about property to the bonds of friendship. The orc way of life is as far removed from us as the dwarves' inclination to live below ground. The orc 'code', the Harrowing, is as remote from human minds as the deeper teachings of the elves. It took me many months to reclaim my humanity when I returned to Hoim, breaking habits I'd learned from the savage tribes, and familiarising myself with the human etiquette I'd cast aside.

Orcs are, by their very nature, a warlike and boisterous lot, able to hack men down with little regard and no regret. They do not pause to reflect or hesitate to con-sider consequence. They not weighed down with think-ing as men are. The prospect of violence calls to the orcs as surely as gold attracts dwarves. And yet it is this great need to do harm that prevents the orcs from prevailing in their wish to rid Naer Evain of all other races. It is my belief that this mindless aggression is self-defeating, for it lacks purpose and objective. It is not enough that the orcs raid the farms and towns of other races; they also turn on each other, in spite of their 'code'. To think of the orcs as one unified mass is to assume that the humans of Hoim, Solari and the Arendsonn Kingdom are all one. It is fallacy.

The orcs are divided, and yet the divisions between the tribes are not the faultlines that shake orc society. The greatest schism is between the *Khagan*, who seek to preserve the old ways, and the shamans, who seem to have some larger scheme, despite their dissembling. That the shamans wield real power is undeniable; that their influence has grown is obvious. This is the great danger present within the orcs. There seems to be a new, unclear, purpose uniting some tribes. Those tribes have shamans who provide objectives for orcs who would not be able to imagine them otherwise. But where does the shaman power come from, and what price are the shamans paying for it? What fell bargains have they agreed for their nascent arcane gifts?

What I came to understand during my time among the orcs was that they are a society in turmoil. Naturally given to a chaotic existence, they are spurred on by the shame of their defeat at the Battle of Salt Wind. It is difficult to fully express the frustration and despair this passage of history has inflicted on the orc psyche. Only the orcs' continued persecution by the elves during the arrival of Khaeris is comparable. Orc minds are rarely preoccupied with the past; they are more fixed on recent times, and events they are better able to comprehend, such as war.

This collective shame is used to manipulate the orcs by the shamans, who attract large retinues of their kin, often placing them in conflict with the *Khagan*. The *Khagan* are not political and are ill-suited to deal with these charismatic and otherworldly personalities. It is my reckoning that only the orcs' respect for tradition, their deep-seated conservatism, protects them from the hidden schemes of the shamans. However, I have no doubt that, in time, tribes led by shamans, not *Khagan*, will roam Naer Evain. This will be the start of a new dark age, even a return to the Shadow War (as the elves call it).

Unlike with elves, one cannot reason with the orc; he cares not for talking. Unlike the dwarf, he cares not for trade. There is nothing he wants that he cannot take from you. Indeed, to barter would feel like a failure to an orc. They are singularly impressed by the rigours of pillaging, boasting of the obstacles they were forced to overcome to acquire each stolen object. In truth, the orc revels in hardship. The orc is as hard-working as humans are given to sloth, ferocious where humans are meek, loyal where we are given to betrayal. Orcs are far from being dark mirrors of men's souls and humans could learn much from orc conduct.

Saying this will undoubtedly make me unpopular, so I eschew special pleading and offer up the orcs' deficiencies, of which I am well aware.

Their lack of artisans and reliance on pillaging means that they are inferior technologically. Siege engines will elude them until they chance upon capturing a team of dwarf engineers. Heavy armour will be makeshift and ill-fitting until they focus more attention on blacksmithing. Even their weapons are poor, rarely sharpened and often antique.

Their lack of horsemanship is perhaps their greatest weakness. There is no greater way to defeat the vast tribes of orcs than on horseback. While expensive, it is my express recommendation we raise and train as many cavalry regiments as the royal coffers allow. I would also suggest sending our best riders to learn from the elves. Tolerating the arrogance and disparagement of those proud warriors would be worth the trade in wisdom and knowledge.

As a society the orcs are consumed with internecine squabbles, although these are almost always short-lived affairs, producing no blood feuds or grudges (something we humans and the dwarves could learn from). That a society should progress is not a concept within orc culture; their way of life has endured for thousands of years, purely because it does not occur to them it could be any other way. There is little sense of wonder about the orc; he is content in each moment, not caring where the next meal is coming from, or concerned how to improve his lot. Orcs simply exist, in this way not unlike some particularly ferocious herd of animals.

These are my last words on the orcs. I hope never to speak of them again, or lay eyes on one of the scarred brutes. That they exist to exterminate all who are different from themselves should be warning enough to all races.

Yours faithfully,
Sebastian Venghaus
Anthropologist Royal, Hoim

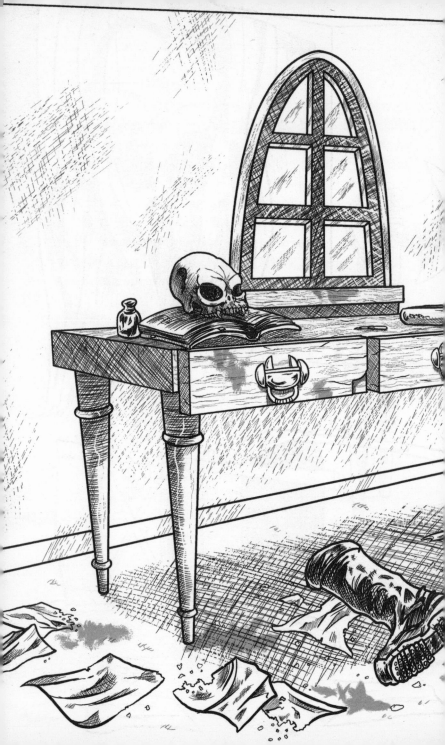

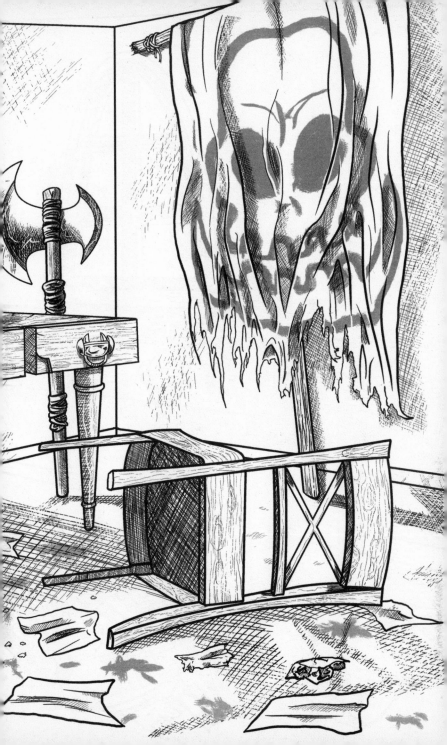